New Compact House Designs

27 Award-Winning Plans
1,250 Square Feet or Less

Edited by Don Metz

STOREY BOOKS
Schoolhouse Road
STOREY Pownal, Vermont 05261

*The mission of Storey Communications is to serve our customers
by publishing practical information that encourages personal independence
in harmony with the environment.*

Cover design by Cindy McFarland
Text design by Judy Eliason

Front and back cover photographs of Washington Island House (p. 30) by Gregory Murphey.

Copyright © 1991 by Storey Communications, Inc.

The information in this book is true and complete to the best of our knowledge. All recommendations are made without guarantee on the part of the author or Storey Books. The author and publisher disclaim any liability in connection with the use of this information. For additional information, please contact Storey Books, Schoolhouse Road, Pownal, Vermont 05261.

Storey Books are available for special premium and promotional uses and for customized editions. For further information, please call Storey's Custom Publishing Department at 1-800-793-9396.

Printed in the United States by Vicks Lithograph
20   19   18   17   16   15

Library of Congress Cataloging-in-Publication Data

New compact house designs : 27 award-winning plans, 1,250 square feet or less / edited by Don Metz.
          p.   cm.
       Includes bibliographical references and index.
       ISBN 0-88266-667-3 (hc) — ISBN 0-88266-666-5 (pb)
        1. Small houses—North America—Designs and plans.   2. Architecture, Domestic—North America—Awards.   I. Metz, Don.
       NA7203.N48   1991
       728'.37'022273—dc20   90-50608
                          CIP

Contents

Introduction

Predicting future housing trends is never easy. What seems inevitable today often becomes a mere footnote to the unforeseen tomorrow. Looking back on the decade since the publication of our first *Compact House Book* in 1983, we find a number of surprises.

For instance, the widely held belief that the size of houses would diminish in response to rising costs and the diminishing number of persons per household never happened. Despite a compelling demography of ever-smaller families, more childless couples, more singles and senior citizens, the average American dwelling unit increased in size by roughly 15 percent during the '80s, reaching a median of 1,850 square feet. (In contrast, the average household in Japan in 1990 contained approximately 850 square feet of living space.)

The rapidly rising cost of land and housing seemed to have no negative effect on sales and encouraged few markets for smaller, less expensive housing units. Although single-family housing starts (attached and detached) varied from a low of 663,000 in 1982 to a high of over 1,140,000 in the boom years of 1986 and 1987, demand for more room and extra niceties never ceased. Another surprise was that the dire predictions of energy shortages and the concomitant development of solar technologies failed to materialize, with the return of inexpensive imported oil in the early 1980s.

The 1990s begin with profound political changes in eastern Europe, the emergence of a depressed world market economy, and chaos in the Middle East oil fields. As we attempt to predict the future once again, we would be foolish not to consider the impact of these global developments as well as the traditional criteria, such as birth rates, employment, land costs, immigration quotas, family patterns, and energy-efficient design. For example, the M.I.T. Center for Real Estate Development reports that the average American household has declined from 4.2 persons in 1940 to 2.3 today. The Urban Land Institute tells us that in 1970 married couples accounted for 71 percent of all households, while today their share has declined to under 57 percent, and the trend continues.

This book is dedicated to the proposition that compact houses have always made good sense. Compact design is built around the idea of stretching space. Rooms borrow space from adjacent rooms, circulation space is minimized, and outside spaces are pulled inside. Every "trick in the book" of efficient planning shows up at least once in the designs found in *New Compact House Designs*. The enthusiasm with which our last volume was received tells us that there is a considerable segment of the population interested in the many advantages of "less is more" housing *despite* conflicting trends and statistics. Although manufactured (compact, mobile) homes now account for over 6 percent of our nation's housing stock, distinctive and imaginative compact house designs are difficult to find. So we went out and found them.

The houses appearing in these pages were chosen from among the many submissions to our second nationwide Compact House Design Competition. Entries flooded in from architects and designers located all across the United States and Canada. The response was enthusiastic, and the exceptional quality of the work received suggests that there are plenty of people out there thinking hard about compact design. Architects Peter Woerner and Don Metz and project editor Ben Watson spent long hours reviewing the merits of each project and finally selected 27 winners, intended to represent a wide variety of tastes, budgets, and site considerations.

The texts and drawings used to describe each project are intended to provide the reader with basic and essential information. Each of the designs, however, is proprietary, and is by right the property of the designers or architects involved. Their names and addresses have been listed in the "Obtaining Information on Plans" section on page 188, and readers are urged to contact them directly. Fees for working drawings and specifications will vary, as will levels of experience. Some of the houses shown in these plans have been built, others are in the process of being built, and still others are waiting for a client — like you. Use this book as a guide to the possible, and then contact the author of your favorite design and make a compact house your own.

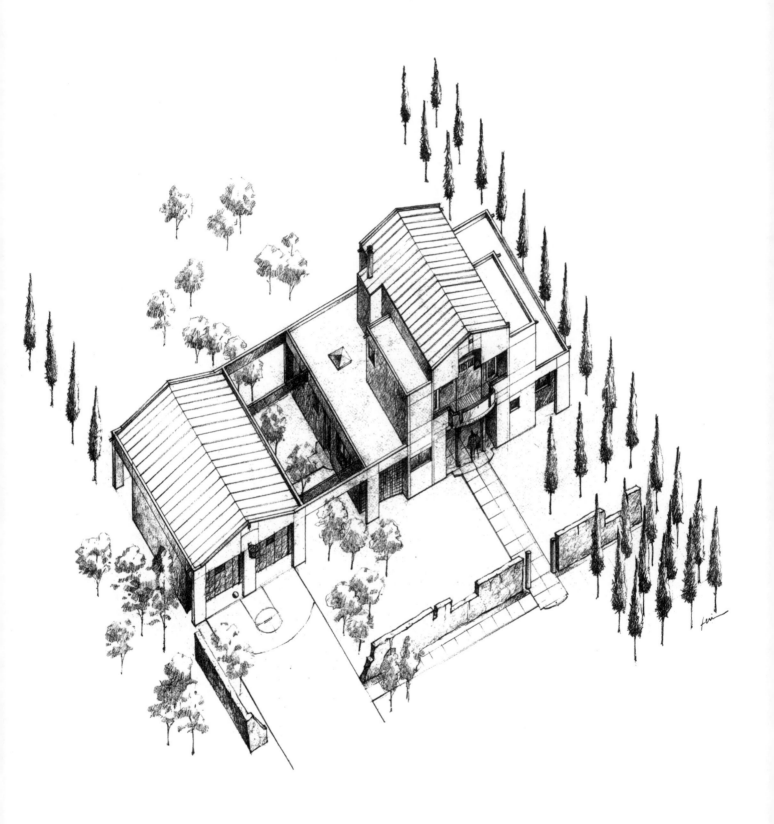

Ferrier

First Prize Winner

Clear, orderly plan. Entry in living room makes a nice space. The kitchen and dining room open onto courtyards, which gives a gestalt to those areas. Uses the garage to make the exterior spaces. Sensitivity to landscaping and exterior site planning.
PETER WOERNER

Elegant, inviting, well-proportioned spaces. The Postmodern touches reach well beyond "style."
DON METZ

Richard B. Ferrier

The basic concepts utilized in the design of this house are: clarity of organization and circulation, zoning according to public and private spaces, and the notion of images which depict dwelling. The plan employs a crossaxial organizational scheme with horizontal planes clearly defining spatial zones.

The front plane of the house enfronts the street with a single layer that reveals subsequent layers beyond. The image suggests two house forms, the primary two-story block for people and the smaller house for vehicles and ancillary functions. Symmetrical devices are used to provide a formal entry and receiving space for visitors. The living area is two stories high, with a balcony above that serves as a small library leading to the master bedroom on the second floor.

The master suite is well away from the children. The library loft allows a pleasant place to read, write, talk on the telephone, or watch the children below. The plan provides for a darkroom adjacent to the library. We have included an alternate plan for this area illustrating how the space might be utilized for additional closet space in the master bath area.

Circulation is at the edge of rooms rather than corridors. It is the variation of spatial definition and different views from the spaces which allow for a variety of experiences.

The auto storage is separated for practical as well as psychological considerations. In rural as well as some urban areas, one can realize a significant savings in insurance if the garage is detached from

TECHNICAL DATA

Gross Square Feet:
1,250

Location:
North-central Texas; adaptable to other sites

Materials:
Wood frame on 2'8" grid, stucco or wood siding; double-insulated wood windows with "E" glass (Andersen); special stained leaded glass as indicated; 6" square glass block; standing seam galvanized metal roof;

metal fascia, gutters, and downspouts; wood, concrete, and tile floors; drywall and tile interior wall finishes; low-voltage halogen lighting; Thermadore or GE white kitchen appliances; Coirian countertops, or plastic laminate; metal recirculating fireplace; Lennox high-efficiency HVAC system, 12 SEER min.; gas-fired heater and water heater, electric cooling

Estimated Cost to Build:
1,250 sq. ft. @ $80.00/sq. ft. = $100,000

Could be constructed for $60.00/sq. ft. with less rigorous detail and alternative material selections: 1,250 @ $60.00/ sq. ft. = $75,000

Estimated Heating/ Cooling Costs: Varies significantly according to region. Lower in urban areas, higher in rural areas. Electricity costs will be approximately 20% less than speculative "builder houses" in the same area

the primary structure. Since the garage is not typically a conditioned space, this becomes the most economical place to provide generous storage areas. The plan we have devised for the auto storage also indicates alternatives for additional features such as a sauna, greenhouse, workshop, or additional storage.

All large glass areas are carefully protected from direct solar radiation by the layering strategy expressed in this design. During summer months, high sun angles are the norm. During the winter months, low sun angles allow for direct light and heat gain. Metal roofs are used because of their long life, reflective qualities, and fire resistance.

Our wood frame structures are designed on a modular unit of 2 feet, 8 inches. This allows for the most efficient use of materials and construction. The illustrations provided depict this house constructed with stucco as the finish material. Vertical wood siding such as cedar would also be a fine exterior finish material for this design.

In very stable soil conditions, economy can be obtained with slab-on-grade construction. It is our preference in most locations to use pier and beam or perimeter beam and pier construction for the foundation.

Richard B. Ferrier

**Perspective:
Entry/Living**

Perspective

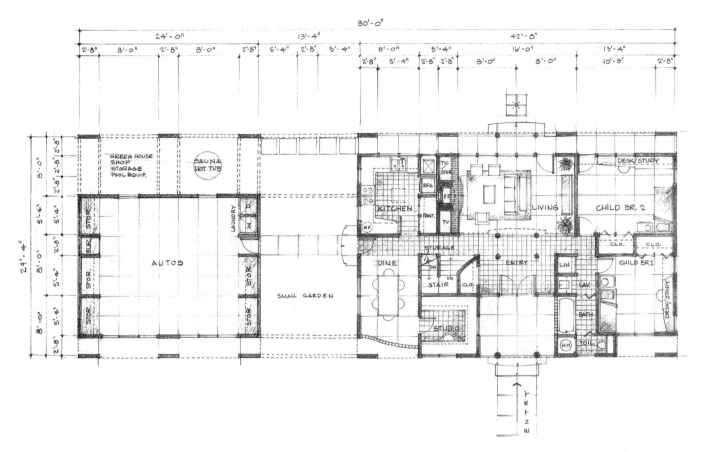

First Floor Plan

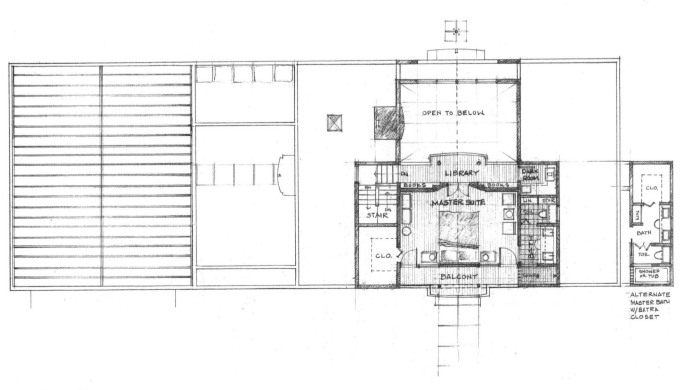

Second Floor Plan

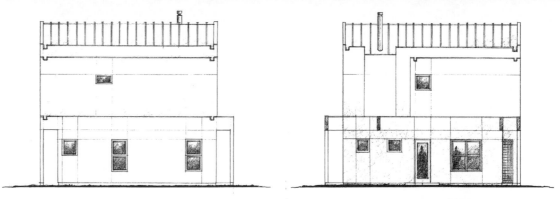

Elevation: Side **Elevation: Side (Kitchen/Dining)**

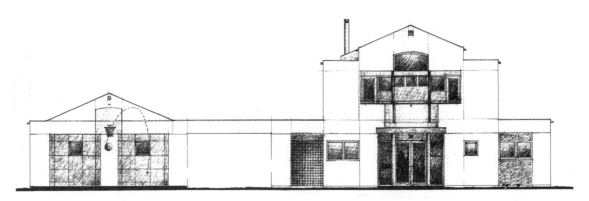

Elevation: Entry/Front

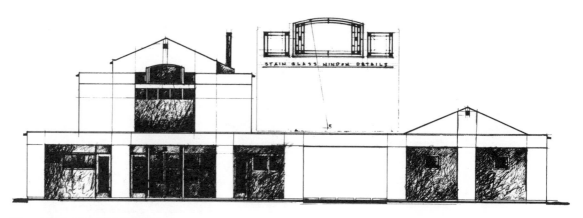

Elevation: Garden/Rear

6

Wall Section

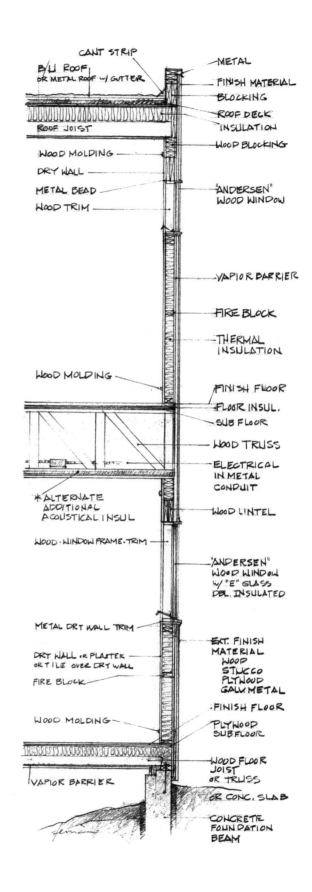

CANT STRIP

B/U ROOF
OR METAL ROOF W/ GUTTER

ROOF JOIST

WOOD MOLDING

DRY WALL

METAL BEAD

WOOD TRIM

WOOD MOLDING

*ALTERNATE
ADDITIONAL
ACOUSTICAL INSUL

WOOD·WINDOW FRAME·TRIM

METAL DRY WALL TRIM

DRY WALL or PLASTER
OR TILE OVER DRY WALL

FIRE BLOCK

WOOD MOLDING

VAPIOR BARRIER

METAL

FINISH MATERIAL

BLOCKING

ROOF DECK

INSULATION

WOOD BLOCKING

"ANDERSEN"
WOOD WINDOW

VAPIOR BARRIER

FIRE BLOCK

THERMAL
INSULATION

FINISH FLOOR

FLOOR INSUL.

SUB FLOOR

WOOD TRUSS

ELECTRICAL
IN METAL
CONDUIT

WOOD LINTEL

"ANDERSEN"
WOOD WINDOW
W/ "E" GLASS
DBL. INSULATED

EXT. FINISH
MATERIAL
WOOD
STUCCO
PLYWOOD
GALV. METAL

FINISH FLOOR

PLYWOOD
SUBFLOOR

WOOD FLOOR
JOIST
OR TRUSS

OR CONC. SLAB

CONCRETE
FOUNDATION
BEAM

Perspective

Rammed Earth Works

Second Prize Winner

Don Callahan

Henri Mannik

David Easton

Jeff Reed

JURY COMMENTS

A delightfully solid, simple, nostalgic design that utilizes an interesting and economical building technology. Better in some climates than others.
DON METZ

Solid, energy-efficient, Old World charm. Site-specific building system.
PETER WOERNER

Comfortable, welcoming, and secure. Outstanding use of niche spaces within the walls to both expand usable work and living areas and create personal "retreats" for privacy.
BEN WATSON

The construction elements are earth and wood.

Environmental responsibility and our commitment to appropriate technologies present us with these timeless materials, and timelessness leads to an architecture not pretentious, but essential.

Feng shui, the ancient Chinese science of creating harmonious architecture, maintains that site, design, and materials must be in balance. To walk through the door into home is to walk into outstretched arms. To watch the sun rise through an eastern window is to cherish the challenges of a new day.

Our essential house, simple yet inspiring, is located in the Napa Valley region of northern California on a narrow, south-facing city lot. The residence derives its strength and functionality in this urban setting from sound-absorbing, monolithic earth walls. These 2-foot-thick walls, in conjunction with active and passive solar systems, retain the warmth of sunny winter days as well as the coolness of the foggy summer nights. Earth walls not only save on heating and cooling costs, but also on maintenance costs. Best of all, a well-built solid masonry house will last for centuries.

Imagine quiet, cozy seats in most windows, niches and bookcases carved from the thick walls, private kid's spaces under the sloping roof, and a kitchen designed to make recycling a natural.

Two thousand years of successful vernacular architecture support these simple solutions: A practical design for comfortable living, massive earth masonry for energy efficiency, and sustainable materials for environmental responsibility.

Rammed Earth Works

TECHNICAL DATA

Gross Square Feet:
1,241 (within 24" walls)

Location:
Napa, California (2,750 degree days)

Materials:
Stabilized rammed earth walls; radiant terratile

flooring; timber second-floor and roof framing; pine tongue-and-groove decking; rigid insulation; composition shingle roof

Type:
Solid masonry/thermal storage

Estimated Cost to Build:
$80,000

Estimated Heating/ Cooling Costs:
$150.00 annually

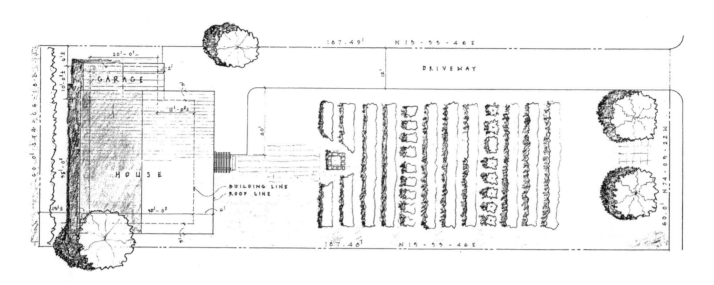

**Installing Radiant
Slab and Earth Tile
Floor**

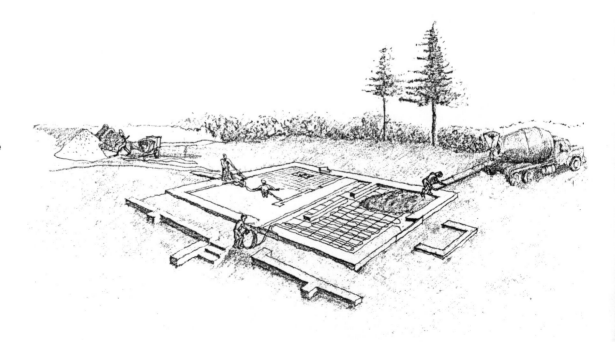

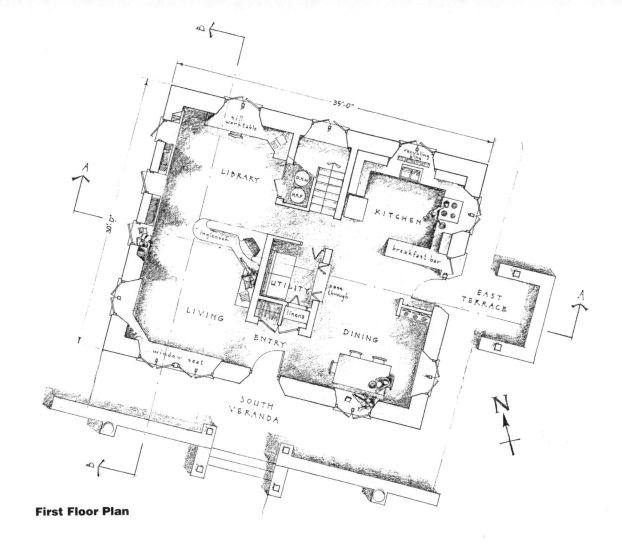

First Floor Plan

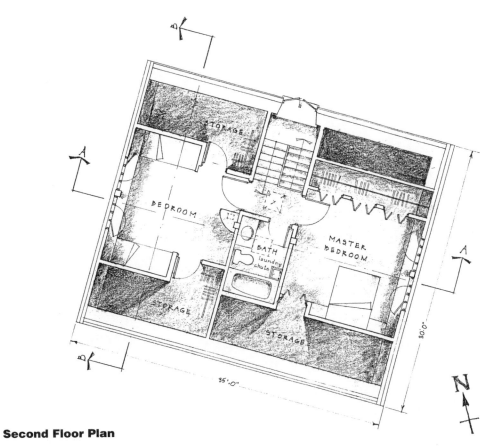

Second Floor Plan

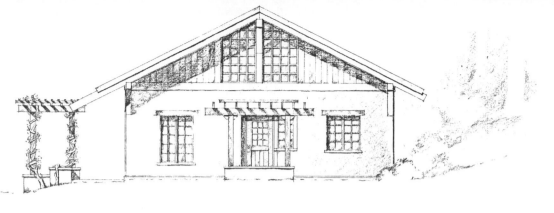

East Elevation

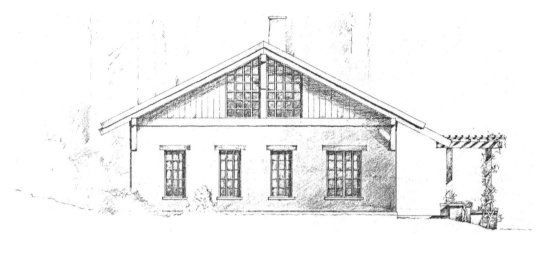

West Elevation

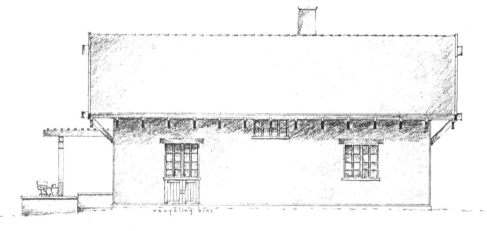

recycling bins

North Elevation

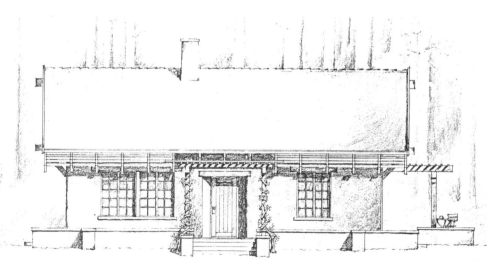

South Elevation

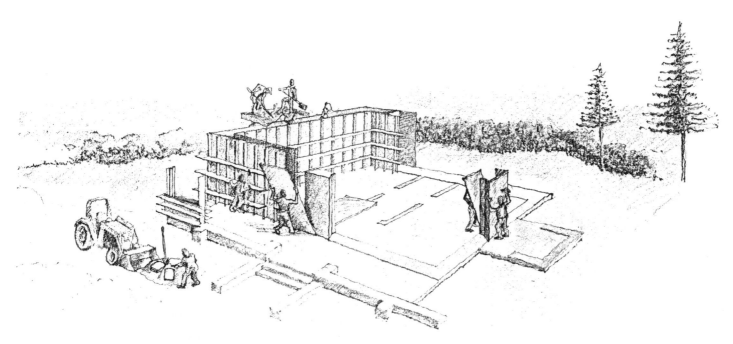

Constructing Solid Earth Walls

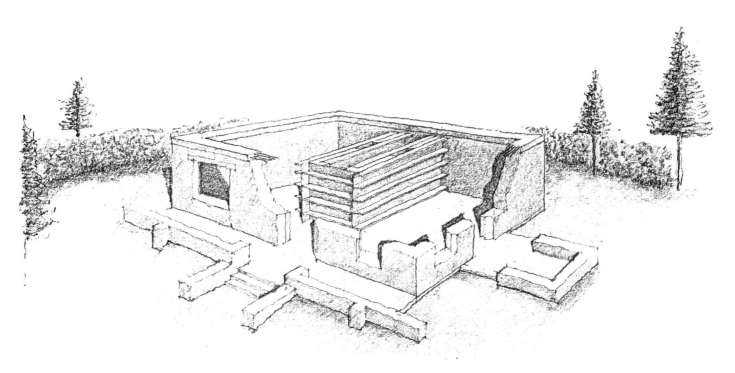

Casting Interior Walls

13

Framing Upper Floor and Roof

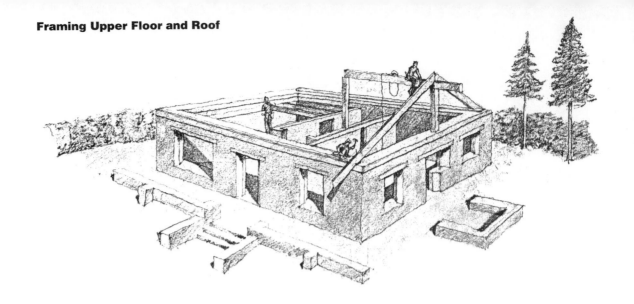

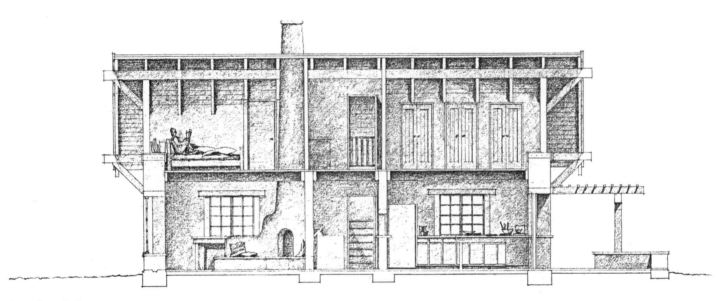

Section A-A

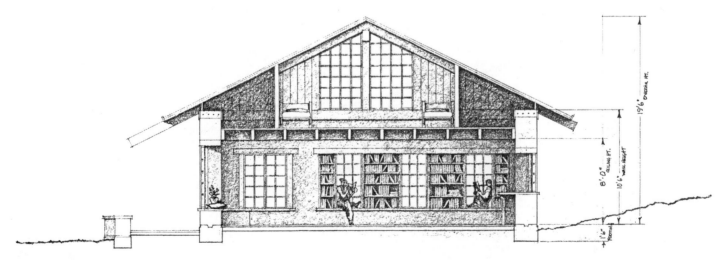

Section B-B

Wall Details

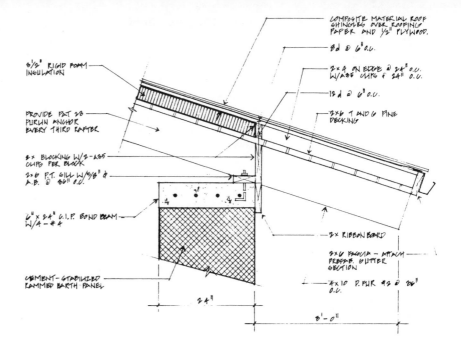

COMPOSITE MATERIAL ROOF SHINGLES OVER ROOFING PAPER AND ½" PLYWOOD.

8d @ 6" O.C.

2×4 ON EDGE @ 24" O.C. W/A35 CLIPS @ 24" O.C.

12d @ 6" O.C.

2×6 T AND G PINE DECKING

3½" RIGID FOAM INSULATION

PROVIDE PA5 28 PURLIN ANCHOR EVERY THIRD RAFTER

2× BLOCKING W/2-A35 CLIPS PER BLOCK

2×6 P.T. SILL W/5/8" Ø A.B. @ 46" O.C.

6" × 24" C.I.P. BOND BEAM W/4-#4

2× RIBBON BOARD

2×6 FASCIA – ATTACH PREFAB. GUTTER SECTION

4×10 D.FIR #2 @ 24" O.C.

CEMENT-STABILIZED RAMMED EARTH PANEL

24"

8'-0"

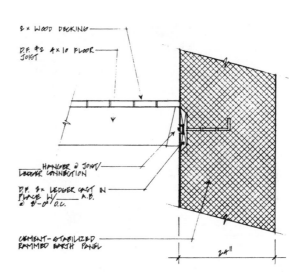

2× WOOD DECKING

D.F. #2 4×10 FLOOR JOIST

HANGER @ JOIST/ LEDGER CONNECTION

D.F. 2× LEDGER CAST IN PLACE W/ A.B. @ 8'-0" O.C.

CEMENT-STABILIZED RAMMED EARTH PANEL

24"

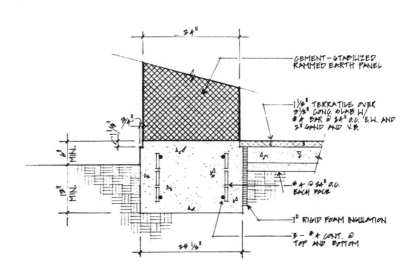

24"

CEMENT-STABILIZED RAMMED EARTH PANEL

1½" TERRATILE OVER 3½" CONC. SLAB W/ #4 BAR @ 24" O.C. E.W. AND 2" SAND AND V.B.

3¾"

6" MIN.

12" MIN.

#4 @ 24" O.C. EACH FACE

1" RIGID FOAM INSULATION

2 – #4 CONT. @ TOP AND BOTTOM

25½"

Perspective

Conde

Third Prize Winner

JURY COMMENTS

Curved roof gives a strong sense to massing. The different shapes to each roof give a strength to the two masses that would be diminished by both being the same. A relatively sophisticated design.
PETER WOERNER

I like the glossy, high-tech lines of the structure, the sureness of the architecture. A warm-climate house, sophisticated and urbane.
DON METZ

Primitivo Emilio Conde

This design is a study in providing an energy-, cost-, and space-efficient house that is responsive to the functional and aesthetic needs of the people that use it. Its spaces intimate and dynamic are intended to romance and excite the users as they experience the routine of daily living.

The centrally located courtyard is the transition of exterior and interior spaces. The courtyard links the living spaces on the ground floor and allows them to expand functionally and visually. Upstairs, the use of a shared tub/shower allows the typical bathroom to double and provide private access from either bedroom. The organization of the house as a single room depth helps minimize circulation and increase cross-ventilation.

South Florida's extensive heat and humidity require a series of design parameters that can at times detract from the overall appearance of the house. An example of this is the limited use of windows. In this design, the energy components are used to embellish the overall appearance:

- elevated floors, large overhangs, and clerestory windows help articulate and balance the overall building form;
- trellises derived from Spanish influence allow for exterior shaded use of courtyards and porches;
- radiant barriers, insulation, and ceiling fans when combined with volume ceilings help create dynamic, energy-efficient spaces.

TECHNICAL DATA

Gross Square Feet:
1,240 (excluding porches)

Location:
South Florida

Materials:
Wood frame construction; cedar siding; standing seam metal roof

Type:
Energy-efficient Florida home using requirements by the Florida Solar Energy Center

Estimated Cost to Build:
1,240 sq. ft. @ $50.00/sq. ft. = 62,000

Estimated Heating/ Cooling Costs:
$0-$80.00 per month; peak use in summer

Materials were used in the construction of the house that would not only help the overall cost but insure its sensitivity to the existing surroundings. This need led to the use of the following materials:

- typical wood frame construction
- exterior wood siding
- standing seam metal roof
- raised wood floors
- open-air screened porches and courtyards

The goal in the overall character of the house was to reach back into history and provide an appearance that is vernacular to the South Florida area. In doing so, the architect hopes to have created a house that meets the needs and aesthetic goals required in today's residental design.

Primitivo Emilio Conde

Site Plan

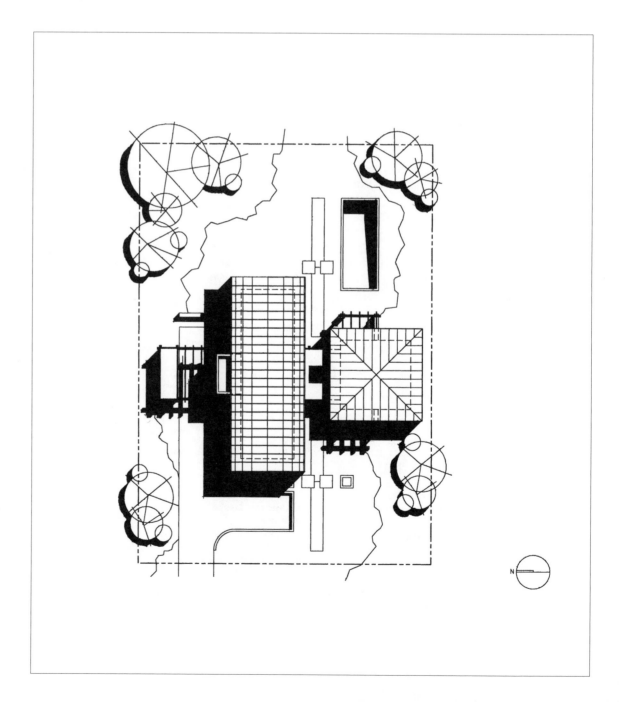

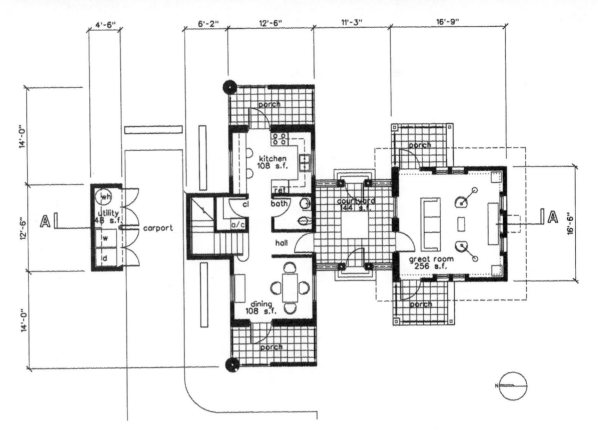

First Floor Plan
780 sq. ft.

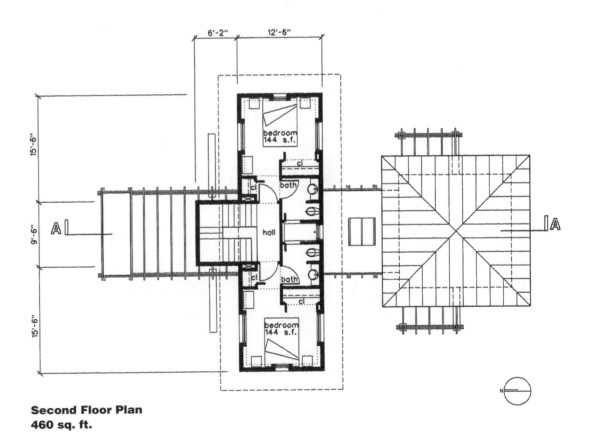

Second Floor Plan
460 sq. ft.

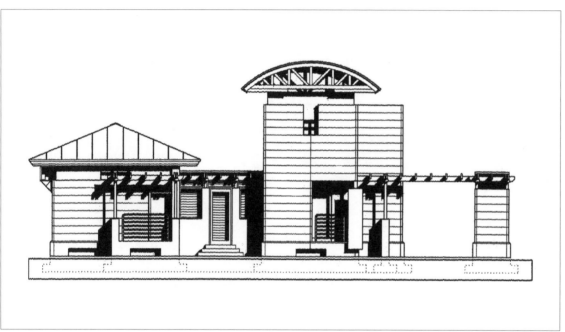

East Elevation

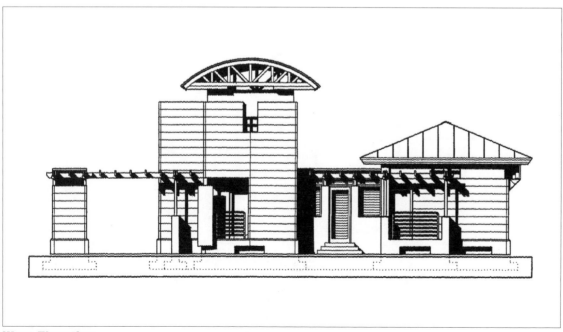

West Elevation

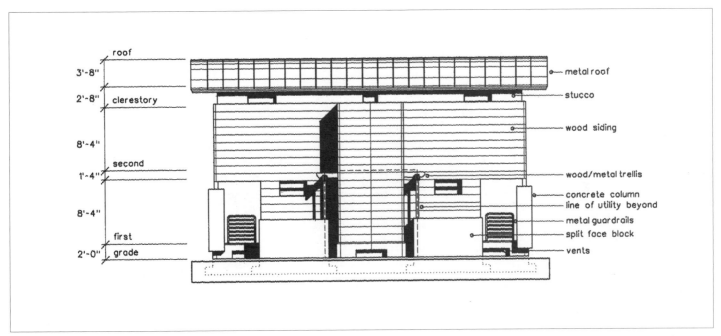

roof		metal roof
3'-8"		
2'-8"	clerestory	stucco
		wood siding
8'-4"		
	second	
1'-4"		wood/metal trellis
		concrete column
8'-4"		line of utility beyond
		metal guardrails
	first	split face block
2'-0"	grade	vents

North Elevation

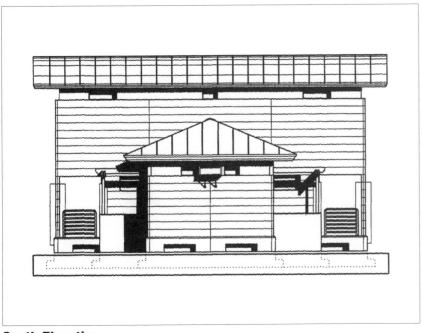

South Elevation

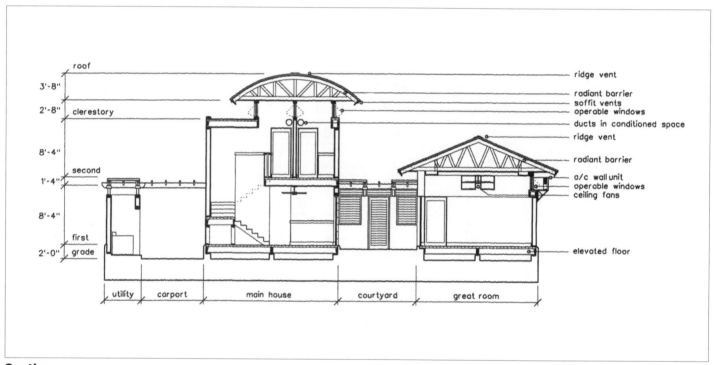

Section

Wall Section

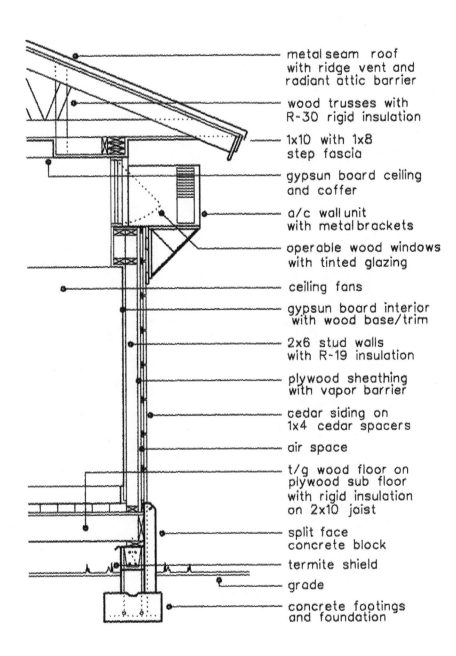

metal seam roof
with ridge vent and
radiant attic barrier

wood trusses with
R-30 rigid insulation

1x10 with 1x8
step fascia

gypsun board ceiling
and coffer

a/c wall unit
with metal brackets

operable wood windows
with tinted glazing

ceiling fans

gypsun board interior
with wood base/trim

2x6 stud walls
with R-19 insulation

plywood sheathing
with vapor barrier

cedar siding on
1x4 cedar spacers

air space

t/g wood floor on
plywood sub floor
with rigid insulation
on 2x10 joist

split face
concrete block

termite shield

grade

concrete footings
and foundation

Perspective

24

Nugent

Jury's Choice Award

A wonderfully compact integration of house and site. A lot of living on a tiny lot.
DON METZ

Courtyard is delightful. Expands a tight site. Great entry; private, yet views beyond. Excellent proportion to living room. Good balconies off of bedrooms. The massing of the house and garage area is handled in a sophisticated way.
PETER WOERNER

Nancy Nugent

CHARLESTON HOUSE

This house is intended as an infill unit for the low-density urban environments so common in the cities of the Southeast. It is loosely based on the Charleston townhouse model with its private garden to the side, as opposed to the rear, of the house. This garden can be defined, as shown with a one-car garage, or simply with a high fence. The large areas of glass facing south onto this garden and the flagstone floor are calculated to give this house passive solar characteristics without looking like a "solar house." The second-story balcony of the master bedroom and deciduous trees shade these openings in summer.

The plan is a simple two room over two room with the stair in between. Mechanical systems are located in a pit below the stairs and share the zero-clearance fireplace flue with the chimney as shown by the minimal masonry chimney.

Of wood frame construction, this house is sided with 6-inch beaded flush siding treated with two coats of deep base stain. The roof is preformed standing seam metal. The windows are true divided-light single panes with insulating interior shutters.

The design of this house is generated from the geometry of the double square. Thus all elements, from the smallest detail to the entire plan and elevations, are unified. This house will evoke in all who experience it a sense of harmony, even though it is of a limited size and scale.

Nancy Nugent

TECHNICAL DATA

Gross Square Feet:
1,250

Location:
Southeastern United States

Materials:
Wood frame construction; concrete footings and foundation; 6" beaded flush wood siding; standing seam metal roof

Estimated Cost to Build:
1,250 sq. ft. @ $80.00/sq. ft. = $100,000

Estimated Heating/Cooling Costs:
N/A

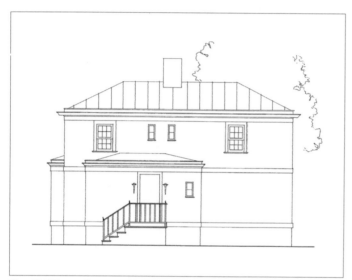

North Elevation

South Elevation

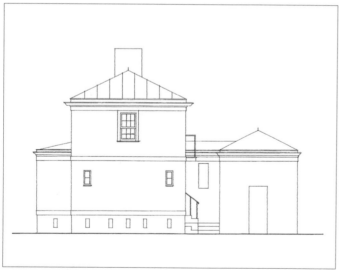

West Elevation

East Elevation

First Floor Plan

Second Floor Plan

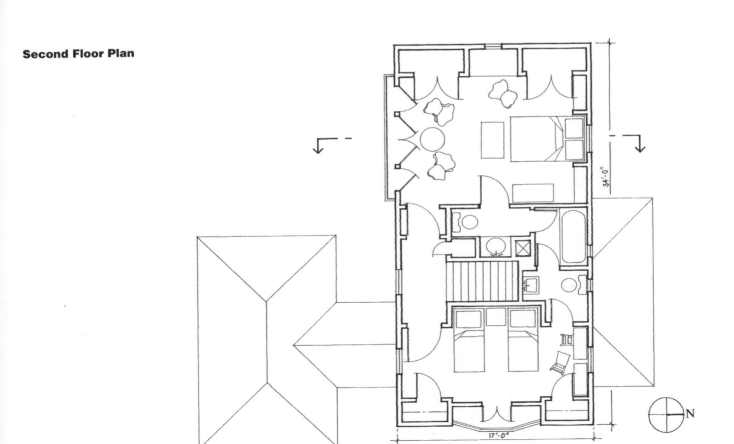

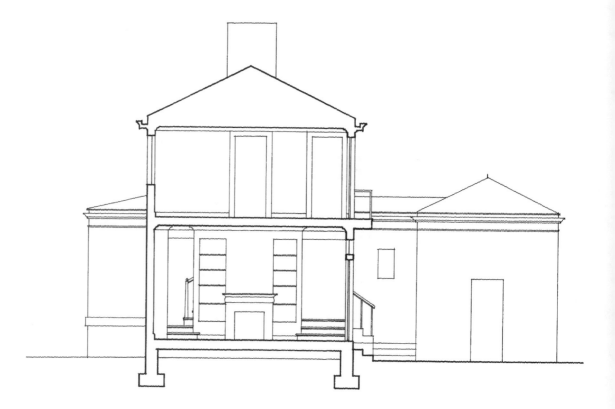

Wall Section

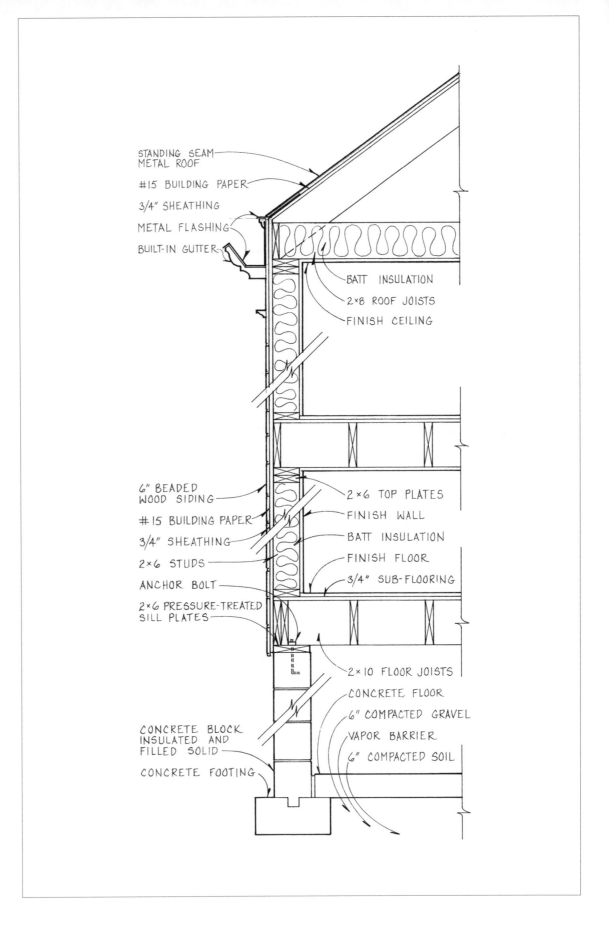

STANDING SEAM METAL ROOF

#15 BUILDING PAPER

3/4" SHEATHING

METAL FLASHING

BUILT-IN GUTTER

BATT INSULATION

2×8 ROOF JOISTS

FINISH CEILING

6" BEADED WOOD SIDING

#15 BUILDING PAPER

3/4" SHEATHING

2×6 STUDS

ANCHOR BOLT

2×6 PRESSURE-TREATED SILL PLATES

2×6 TOP PLATES

FINISH WALL

BATT INSULATION

FINISH FLOOR

3/4" SUB-FLOORING

2×10 FLOOR JOISTS

CONCRETE FLOOR

6" COMPACTED GRAVEL

VAPOR BARRIER

6" COMPACTED SOIL

CONCRETE BLOCK INSULATED AND FILLED SOLID

CONCRETE FOOTING

Perspective
(Axonometric)

30

Phillips

Jury's Choice Award

Good plan. Dynamic exterior spatial sense created by separating bedrooms, bath, and silo.
PETER WOERNER

The scale says "small," but the effective usability is large. A nice relationship of forms and the space between.
DON METZ

Frederick Phillips

This house is inspired in part by typical farm complexes of northern coastal Wisconsin. Three structures house living spaces, bedrooms, and bathrooms, respectively.

The separation of this tiny program (1,200 square feet) into three distinct structures establishes a reassuring community of buildings on this remote 13-acre site on Lake Michigan. Accordingly, this design is as much about the spaces between buildings as it is about the buildings themselves.

Frederick Phillips

TECHNICAL DATA

Gross Square Feet:
1,200

Location:
Washington Island,
Wisconsin

Materials:
#1 red cedar shingles; clear
pine siding; Onduline
asphalt roofing

Type:
Wood frame

**Estimated Cost
to Build:**
1,200 sq.ft. @ $85.00/sq. ft.
= $102,000

**Estimated Heating/
Cooling Costs:**
N/A

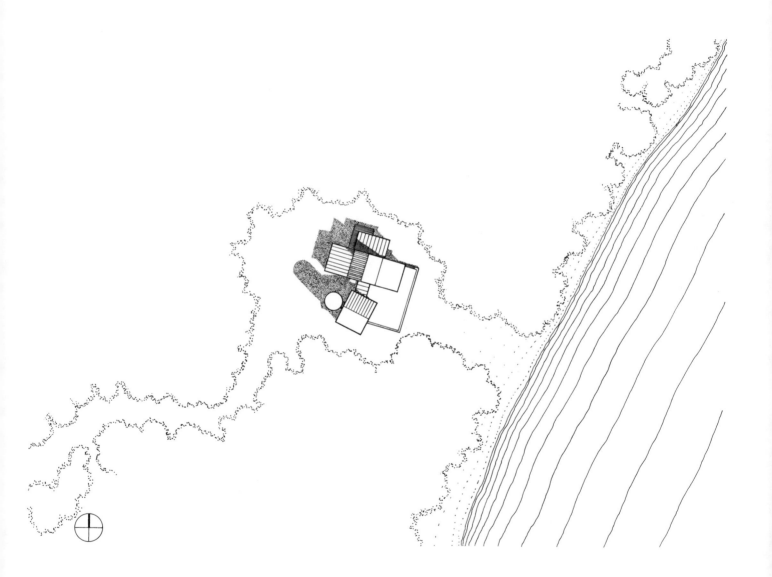

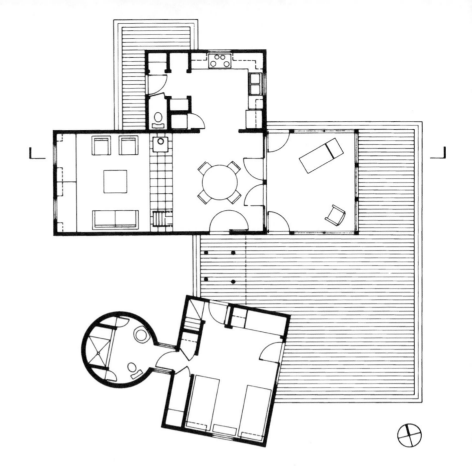

First Floor Plan

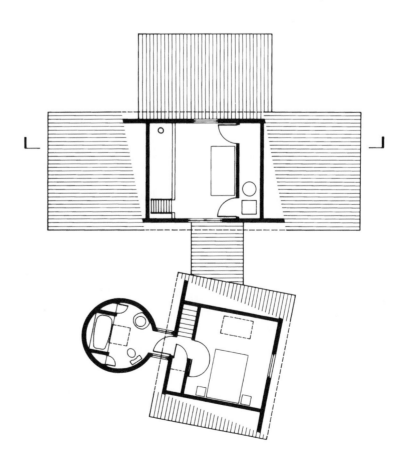

Second Floor Plan

33

East Elevation 1

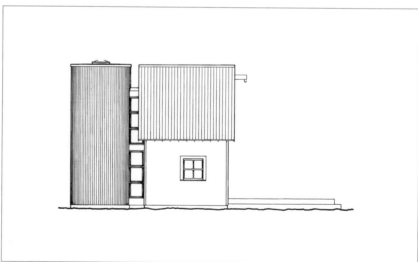

North Elevation 1

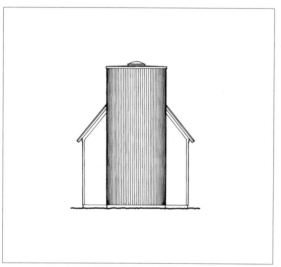

West Elevation 1

South Elevation 1

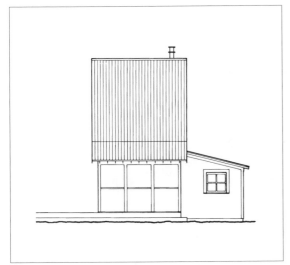

East Elevation 2

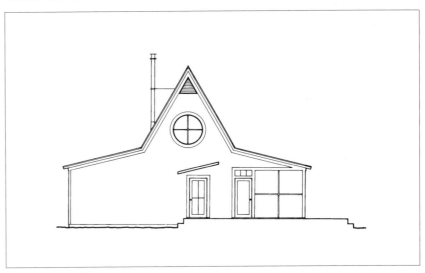

North Elevation 2

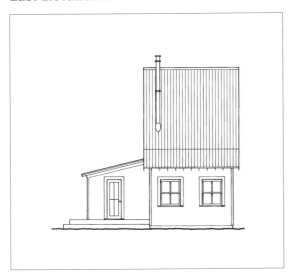

West Elevation 2

South Elevation 2

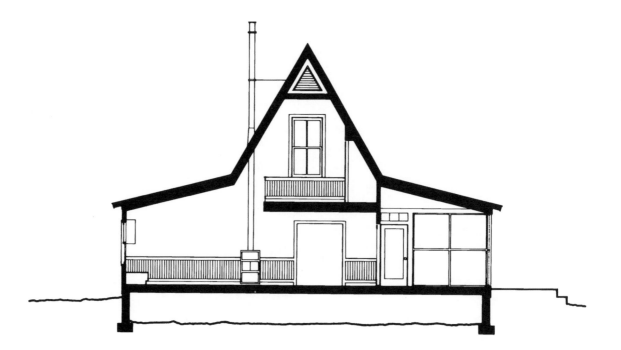

Wall Section

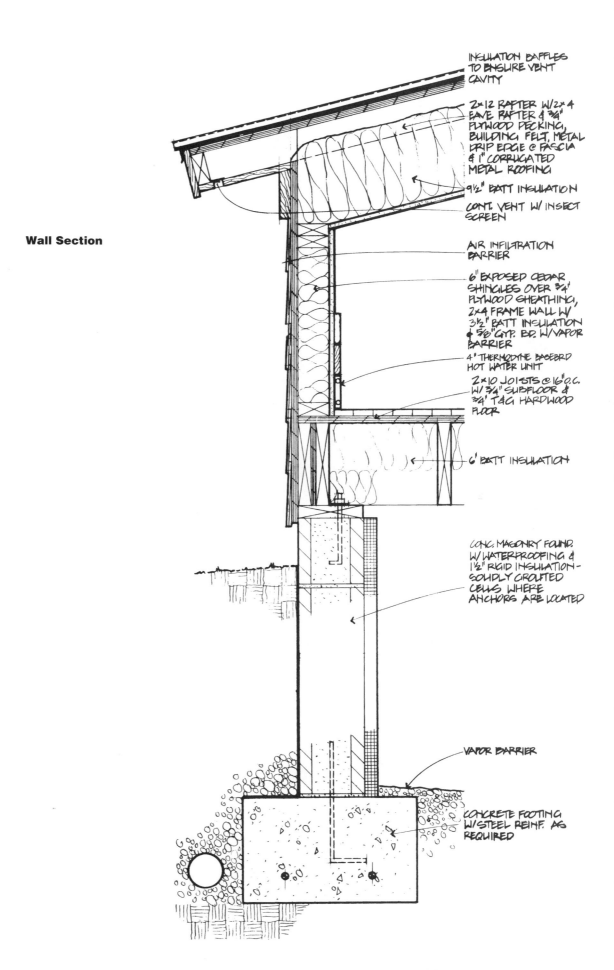

INSULATION BAFFLES TO ENSURE VENT CAVITY

2×12 RAFTER W/2×4 EAVE RAFTER & ¾" PLYWOOD DECKING, BUILDING FELT, METAL DRIP EDGE @ FASCIA & 1" CORRUGATED METAL ROOFING

9½" BATT INSULATION

CONT. VENT W/ INSECT SCREEN

AIR INFILTRATION BARRIER

6" EXPOSED CEDAR SHINGLES OVER ¾" PLYWOOD SHEATHING, 2×4 FRAME WALL W/ 3½" BATT INSULATION & ⅝" GYP. BD. W/VAPOR BARRIER

4" THERMODYNE BASEBRD HOT WATER UNIT

2×10 JOISTS @ 16" O.C. W/ ¾" SUBFLOOR & ¾" T&G HARDWOOD FLOOR

6" BATT INSULATION

CONC. MASONRY FOUND. W/ WATERPROOFING & 1½" RIGID INSULATION - SOLIDLY GROUTED CELLS WHERE ANCHORS ARE LOCATED

VAPOR BARRIER

CONCRETE FOOTING W/STEEL REINF. AS REQUIRED

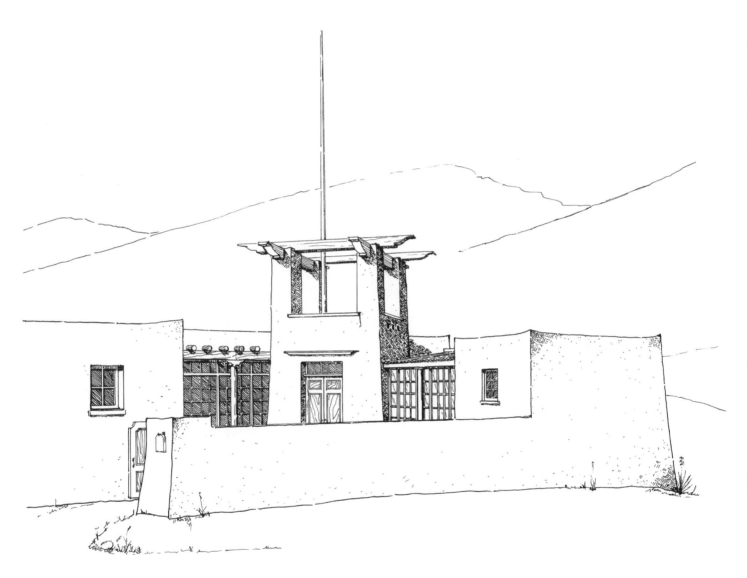

Perspective

Sammons

Jury's Choice Award

Wonderful courtyard. Clear plan. Exciting walk-through entry. This house is more than the sum of its parts due to the courtyard. This house could work anywhere — could be done in wood as well as adobe.

PETER WOERNER

I like how the house wraps around the courtyard, and I like the tower and the internal zoning. An exceptionally nice solution.

DON METZ

Richard Sammons

This 1,220 square foot house was designed for the outskirts of a small town near Santa Fe, New Mexico. It is situated at the corner of two dirt roads that come together at an obtuse angle. The southwest walls of the house follow the line of the roads. Following the lead of John Gaw Meem, the great Santa Fe architect of the beginning of this century, the design freely adapts the local vernacular, in plan and detail.

The house is built of adobe, with the principal rooms opening to the courtyard. One enters through a tower, which can be reached by a steep stair in the vestibule. Inexpensive adobe fireplaces give focus to both the dining and living rooms, and the south-facing window-wall of the latter gives the house some passive solar possibilities. Awnings provide shade and outdoor living in the summer. Primary heating and mechanical systems are situated in a pit below the tower. Air conditioning is not necessary. The perimeter walls have small openings, which focus attention into the courtyard.

Richard Sammons

TECHNICAL DATA

Gross Square Feet:
1,220

Materials:
Adobe stucco over adobe; piñon pine (kitchen) and corrugated steel roofing; wood windows and doors; sandstone pavers in courtyard

Type:
Adobe

Estimated Cost to Build:
1,220 sq. ft. @ $90.00/sq. ft. = $109,800

Estimated Heating/ Cooling Costs:
N/A

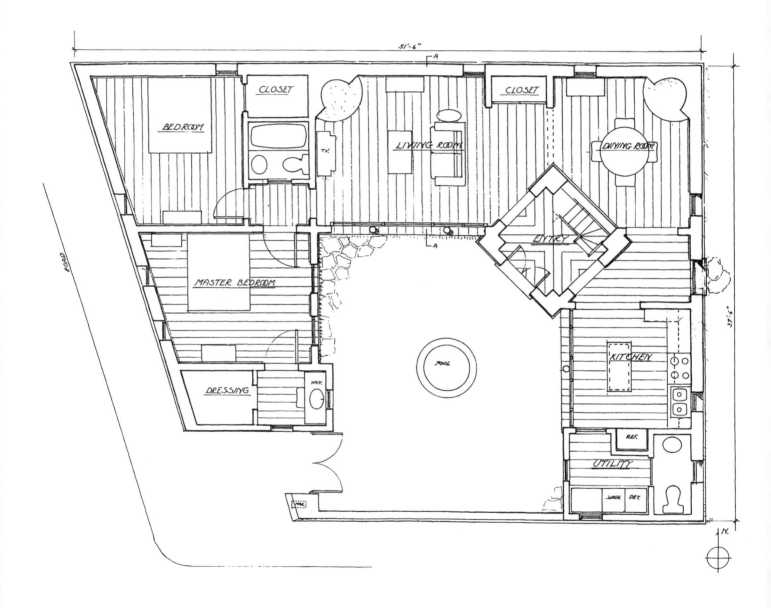

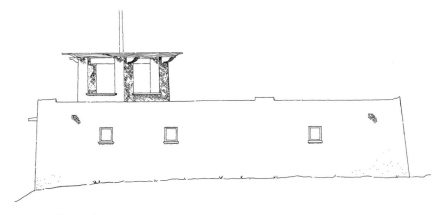

North Elevation

South Elevation

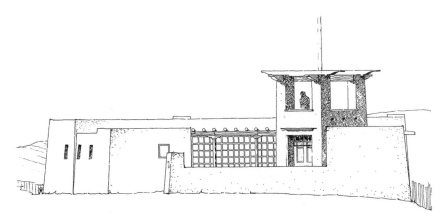

East Elevation

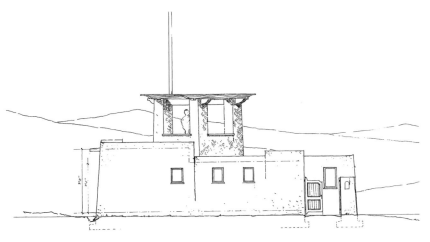

West Elevation

41

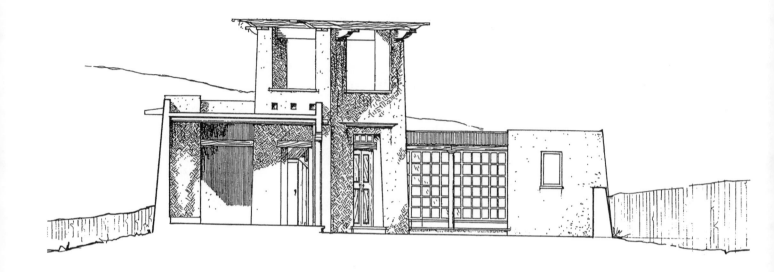

Wall Section

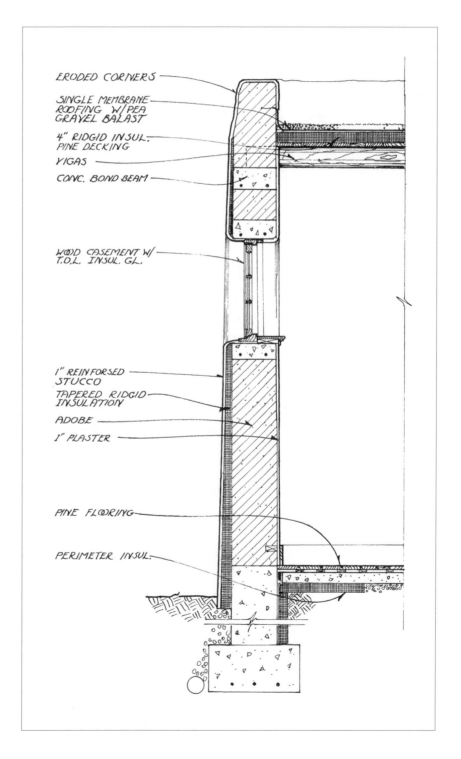

ERODED CORNERS

SINGLE MEMBRANE ROOFING W/ PEA GRAVEL BALAST

4" RIDGID INSUL. PINE DECKING

VIGAS

CONC. BOND BEAM

WOOD CASEMENT W/ T.D.L. INSUL. GL.

1" REINFORSED STUCCO

TAPERED RIDGID INSULATION

ADOBE

1" PLASTER

PINE FLOORING

PERIMETER INSUL.

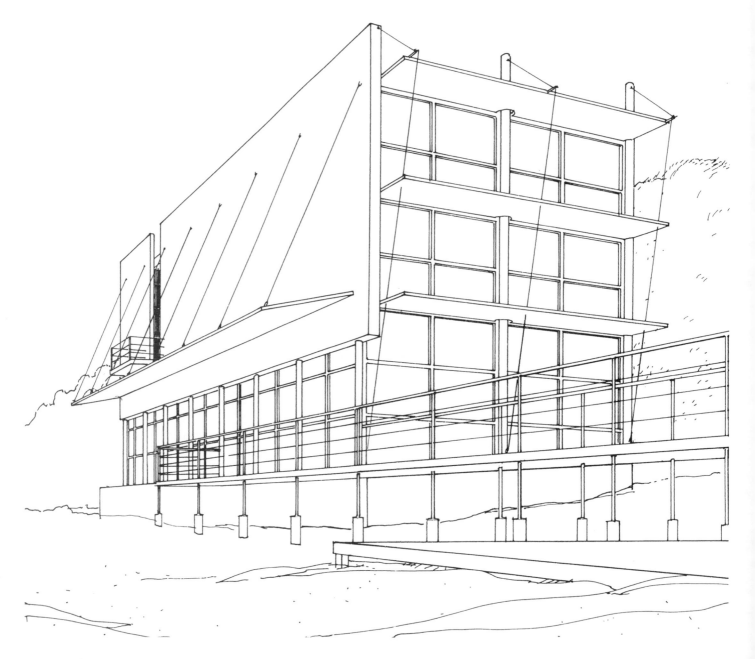

Perspective

Bolsega

Conceptual clarity, big on space, urbane, high-tech elegant, Miesian. A cross between a pavilion and an elegant factory/loft renovation.
DON METZ

Very sophisticated. Fabulous as a place for a couple. Great sense of two-story space — dramatic. The exterior space relationships can be expanded to land, terraces, etc.
PETER WOERNER

Gerard Bolsega

The goal of the compact house is not to "compact" but to expand. The conventional house form with its numerous partitions cuts up space and works against a feeling of expansiveness, especially within a 1,250 square foot compact house program. This house scheme finds its beginning point in these issues and resolves them within its architectural concept.

The plan is long and rectilinear. Within this volume, a great space is kept, and distance itself serves to isolate areas of the house. The functions of kitchen and bath form a core placed so as to act itself as a divider of space. The expansive sense is enhanced by the "floating" of the upper level. Double-high space moves continuously around the perimeter of the house's interior. Space flows horizontally and vertically.

Another key element is the use of large glazed exterior walls. Sandwiched between the lakefront and a grove of trees, the sun-shaded glazed walls allow the interplay of interior and exterior space. The house is not so much a defined, limited enclosure but rather a place within and expanding into its natural setting.

Gerard Bolsega

TECHNICAL DATA

Gross Square Feet:
1,205

Location:
Clear Lake, California

Materials:
Steel, glass, cement, plaster

Type:
Steel frame

Estimated Cost to Build (1990):
$143,800

Estimated Heating/ Cooling Costs:
$1,230

45

Site Plan

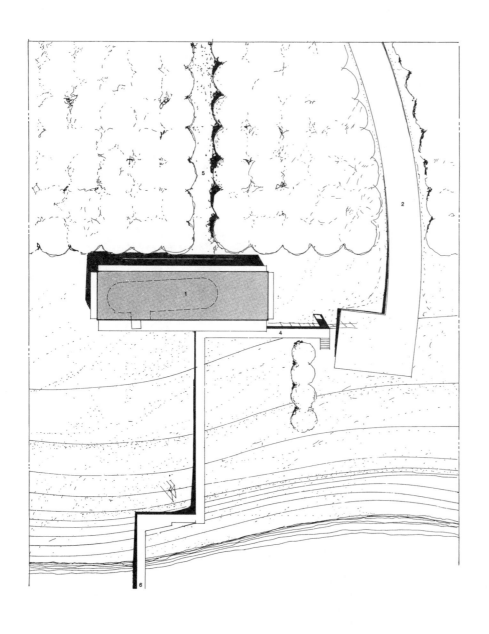

1	HOUSE
2	DRIVE
3	LAKE
4	WALKWAY
5	GROVE OF TREES
6	PIER

1. Entry
2. Living Area
3. Kitchen
4. Multi-Use
5. Storage/Utility
6. Bath
7. Sleeping Area
8. Open to Below
9. Terrace

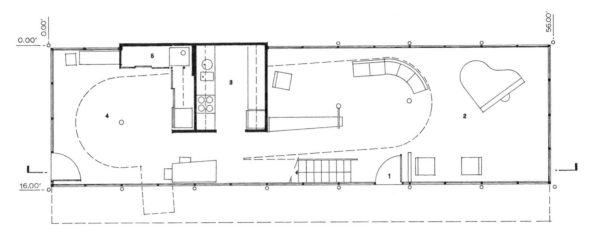

Ground Floor Plan

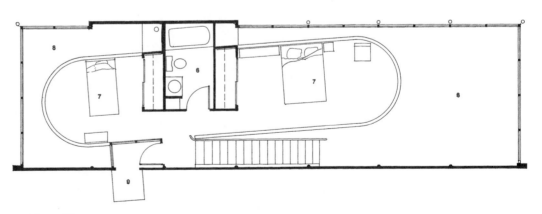

Upper Floor Plan

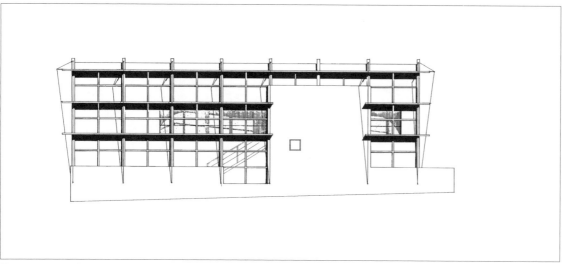

North Elevation

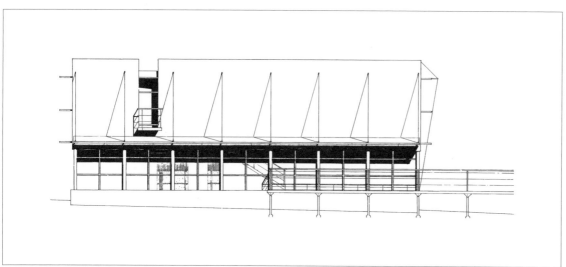

South Elevation

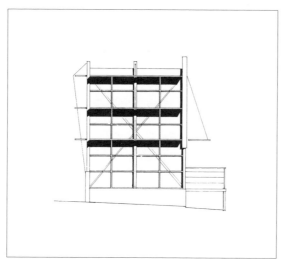

Side Elevation

48

Wall Section

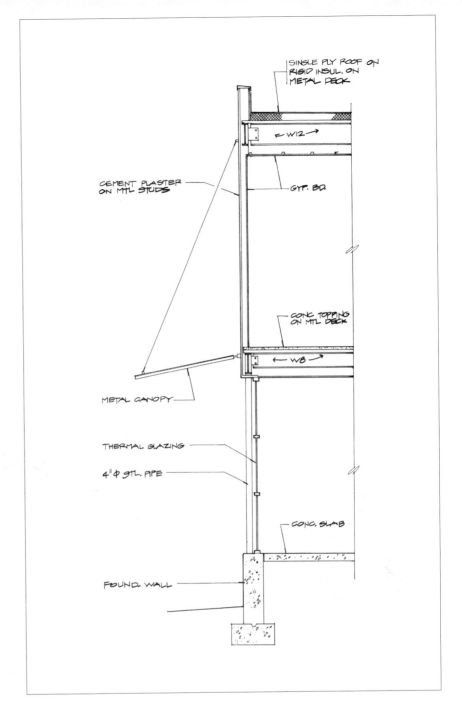

SINGLE PLY ROOF ON RIGID INSUL. ON METAL DECK

← W12 →

CEMENT PLASTER ON MTL STUDS

GYP. BD.

CONC TOPPING ON MTL DECK

← W8 →

METAL CANOPY

THERMAL GLAZING

4" ∅ STL. PIPE

CONC. SLAB

FOUND. WALL

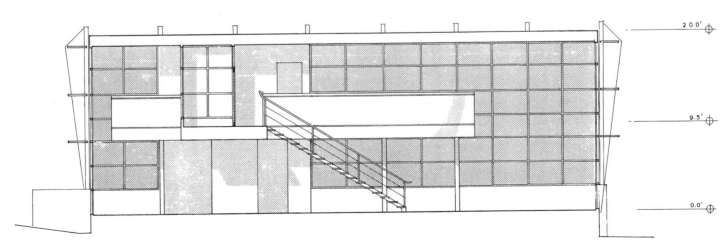

20.0'

9.5'

0.0'

Building Section

Perspective

Burton

JURY COMMENTS

Very exciting. Great expansiveness — expensive to build with large amounts of exterior surfaces. Refreshing. Roof pattern could be manipulated a la "Bruce Goffe" for some major drama.
PETER WOERNER

Nice evocation of the chambered nautilus form. Curves create a dynamic flow of space — worth the extra cost.
DON METZ

Jeffrey Burton

The residence for a design professional couple is situated on a densely wooded 5-acre site in central Florida. It is currently under construction as an owner-builder project with a hard cost estimate of $48.00 per square foot.

The 1,175 square foot, two bedroom, two bath home-studio radiates from a spiral, central living area. Conventional trusses of uniform pitch and varying height and length span the living room by way of a steel "moment transference ring," allowing a central shaft of light to complement the perimeter clerestory.

A recessed floor allows seating around the low table.

The master bedroom opens onto a patio built around an existing palm tree. The master bath's sunken tub features floor-to-ceiling glass facing a private garden.

The powder room becomes a "ship's bath," with a floor drain and tiled walls with a shower head.

Windows encompass the studio area on three sides. A fireplace provides warmth during brisk winter mornings.

A V-grooved stucco exterior wall finish, rough-sawn red cedar fascia and metal roofing, and native co-quina floor tile combine with the formal and spatial experience to produce an organic statement in a subtropic forest.

Jeffrey Burton

TECHNICAL DATA

Gross Square Feet:
1,175

Location:
Black Hammock area,
northeast of Orlando, Florida

Materials:
Cedar fascia, posts, and
trim; standing seam metal
roof; stucco on exterior
insulation system; coquina
tile

Type:
2"x4" frame

**Estimated Cost
to Build:**
$56,400

**Estimated Heating/
Cooling Costs:**
$90.00

*Architectural Renderings by
James Jerris, Orlando,
Florida*

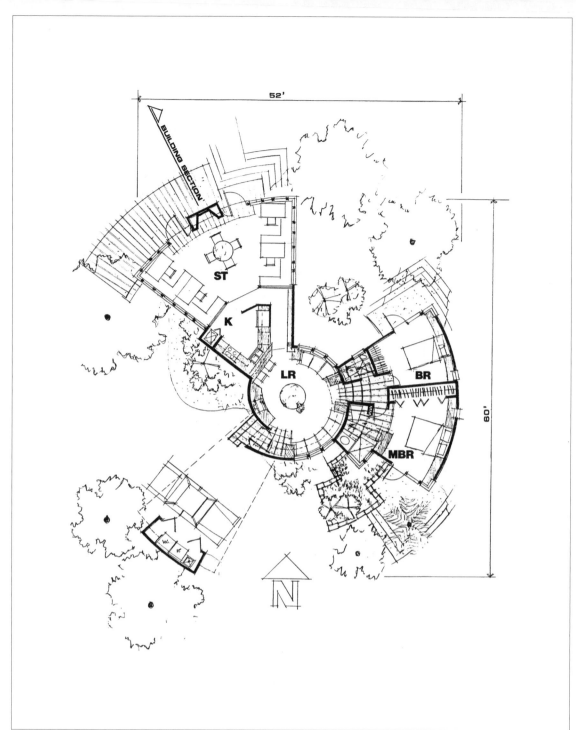

Floor Plan

East Elevation

West Elevation

North Elevation

South Elevation

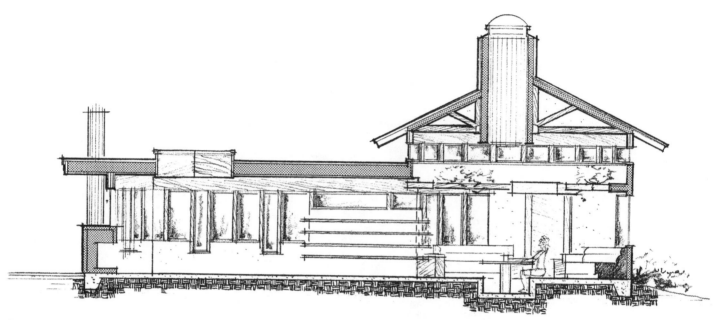

Section

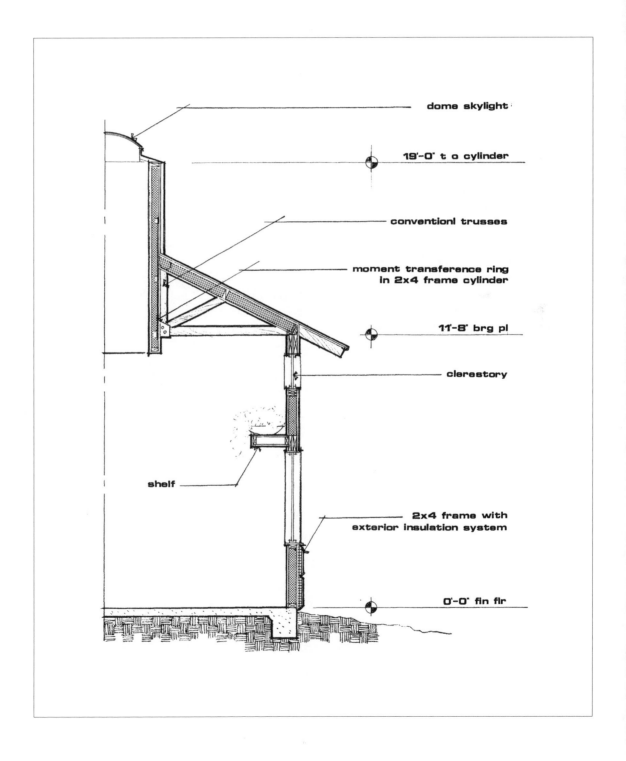

dome skylight

19'-0" t o cylinder

conventionl trusses

moment transference ring
in 2x4 frame cylinder

11'-8" brg pl

clerestory

shelf

2x4 frame with
exterior insulation system

0'-0" fin flr

Perspective

Connor

An attractive, energy-efficient solution for a south-sloping site. Fire resistance, acoustical serenity, and low maintenance are a plus.
DON METZ

Nice linear plan, opening to terrace. The minimal entry gives a great sense of surprise when you descend and the house unfolds.
PETER WOERNER

Michael Clark Connor

This project was conceived in response to the call for submissions to the Second Compact House Competition. The house is not built; there is no specific location, site, or client.

I submitted this design in order to communicate some strongly held beliefs. Among these is that efficiency is valuable in and of itself. When one builds, whether to provide low-cost housing or a piece of expensive architecture, one has a moral obligation not to be wasteful. This is a basic tenet of my personal philosophy of architecture.

Another strongly held belief embodied in this design is that one should choose quality rather than quantity. My fictitious clients would like to build three bedrooms and two baths all at once and not have to

deal with limited space, but to do so they would have to sacrifice quality. My design represents an acceptable alternative to this problem. The compact, efficient core design allows for incremental expansion. Delayed gratification versus instant gratification has, in the end, its own rewards.

Finally, in terms of environmental cost, the issue of energy efficiency is of great concern to all of us. This home relies on a number of passive design strategies in order to be energy-efficient. Primary among these is the placement of the house into a south-facing slope. Important, too, is the use of trees and overhangs to regulate seasonal solar gain.

Michael Clark Connor

TECHNICAL DATA

Gross Square Feet:
1,250 (house)
1,200 (garage)
2,450 (gross)

Location:
Nonspecific

Materials:
Concrete, metal, wood, and glass

Type:
Poured-in-place concrete construction

Estimated Cost to Build:
$90.00/sq. ft. to $110.00/sq. ft. ($112,500 to $137,500 for house; varies with location)

Estimated Heating/ Cooling Costs:
N/A

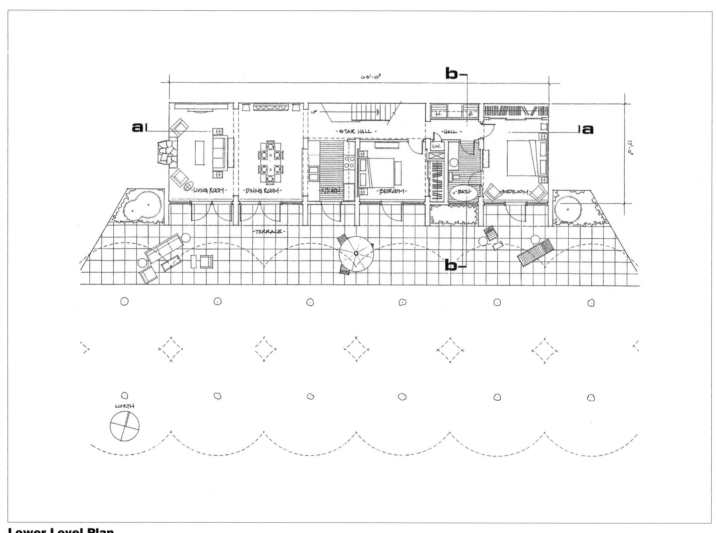

Lower Level Plan

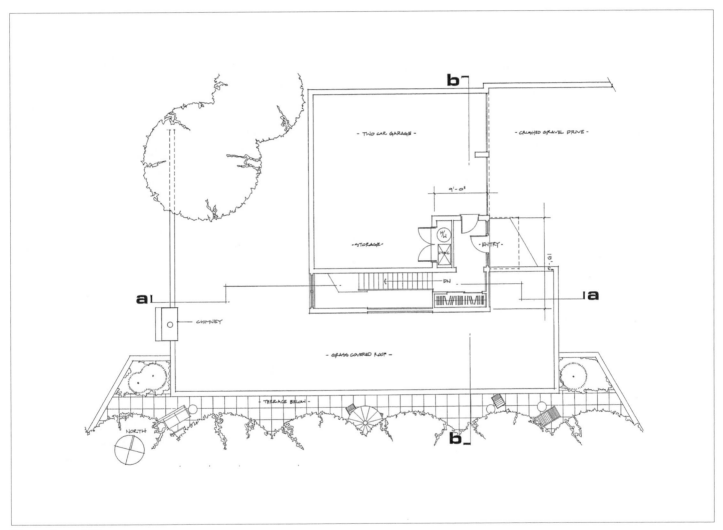

Upper Level Plan

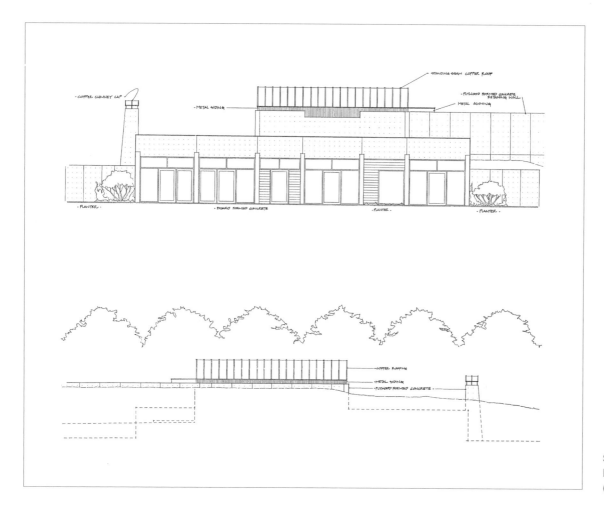

South Elevation (top)
North Elevation
(bottom)

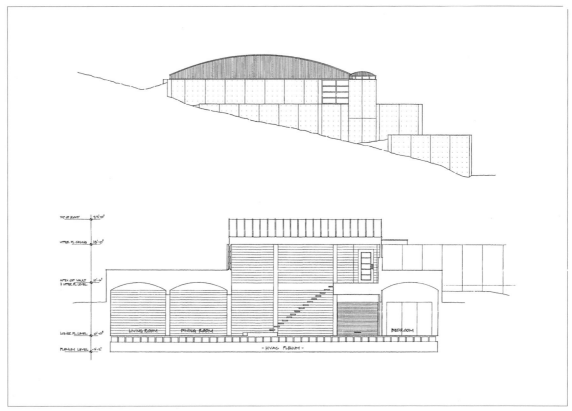

West Elevation (top)
Section A-A (bottom)

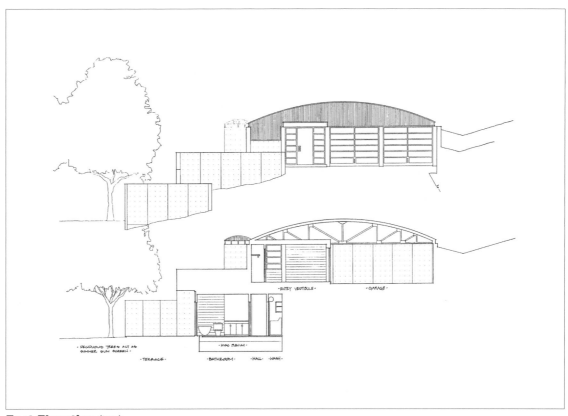

East Elevation (top)
Section B-B (bottom)

Site Plan

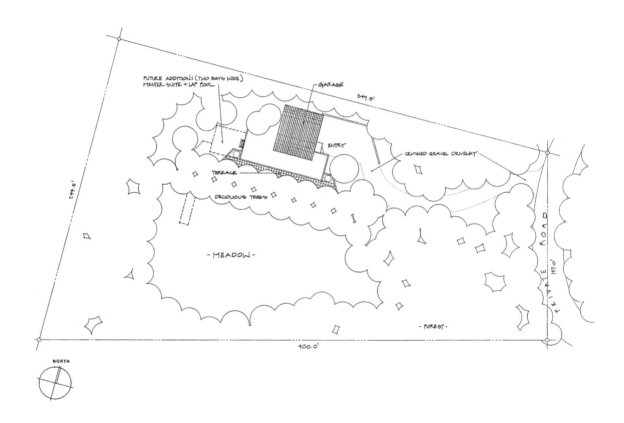

FUTURE ADDITION: (TWO BAYS WIDE)
MASTER SUITE + LAP POOL

GARAGE

349.5'

ENTRY

CRUSHED GRAVEL DRIVEWAY

TERRACE

DECIDUOUS TREES

247.5'

- MEADOW -

147.0'

PRIVATE ROAD

- FOREST -

400.0'

NORTH

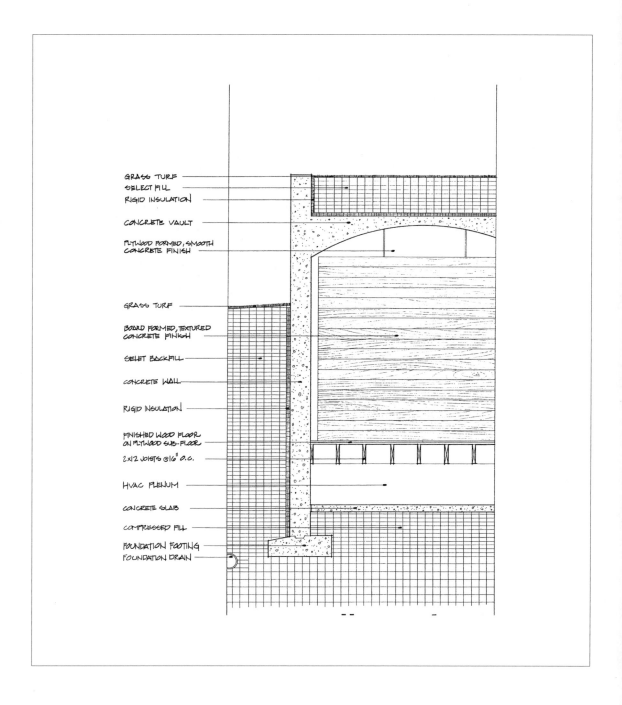

GRASS TURF
SELECT FILL
RIGID INSULATION

CONCRETE VAULT

PLYWOOD FORMED, SMOOTH
CONCRETE FINISH

GRASS TURF

BOARD FORMED, TEXTURED
CONCRETE FINISH

SELECT BACKFILL

CONCRETE WALL

RIGID INSULATION

FINISHED WOOD FLOOR
ON PLYWOOD SUB-FLOOR

2x12 JOISTS @16" O.C.

HVAC PLENUM

CONCRETE SLAB

COMPRESSED FILL

FOUNDATION FOOTING
FOUNDATION DRAIN

Perspective

64

Corkill

JURY COMMENTS

Plan works well — open, exterior deck. Needs expanded use of exterior to maximize its potential.
PETER WOERNER

Big little house with a nice arrangement of spaces. Open first floor plan exemplifies "borrowed space" concept. Good internal zoning.
DON METZ

James M. Corkill

This residence is designed to meet the needs of the first-time buyer and the retired couple buying their last home. Its design is such that it will blend with the contemporary styling of adjacent homes and yet maintain some of the traditional characteristics found in homes throughout the southern and western parts of our country.

The materials used in the design give the homeowner many of the luxuries found in a more expensive home. The home achieves a much larger appearance through the use of varying roof heights, the slope of the roof, and the horizontal lines produced by the siding.

Economic considerations being important, a water source heat pump is used to provide for the heating and cooling as well as the hot water requirements. The fireplace in the living area should also be integrated into the heating system. Awning windows are positioned to provide for cross-ventilation of the home during the spring and fall months. These windows, in conjunction with the open floor plan, do not confine one's eyes to a small area but allow them to visit all parts of the living area.

The residence is divided into the sleeping area upstairs and the living area on the first level. The living area with its open plan allows for freedom of movement. The use of a patio door in the living room brings the out-of-doors inside and makes the room appear more spacious and comfortable.

The use of wood flooring throughout the majority of the house adds a feeling of warmth and continuity to the home. The wood floors also allow for the use of area rugs to accent different sections within the home.

James M. Corkill

TECHNICAL DATA

Gross Square Feet:
1,222

Location:
Designed for southern and western regions of the United States

Materials:
2"x6" framing on a concrete foundation; standing seam metal roof; horizontal wood siding on exterior; Sheetrock for paper or paint on interior

Type:
Wood frame

Estimated Cost to Build:
$58,656

Estimated Heating/ Cooling Costs:
$1,680 per year

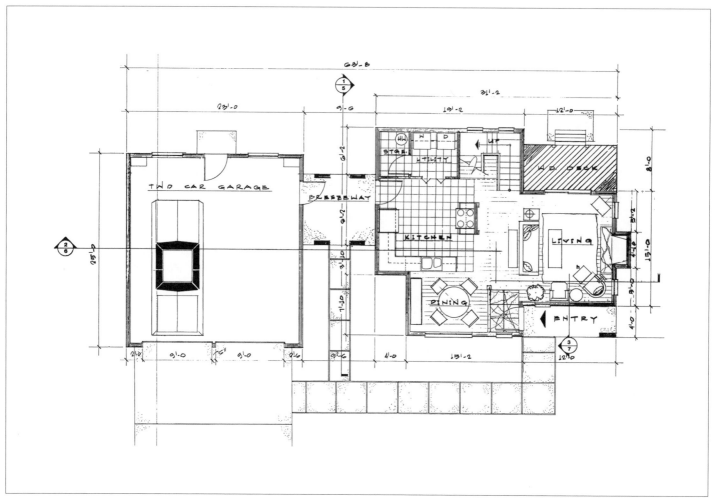

First Floor Plan

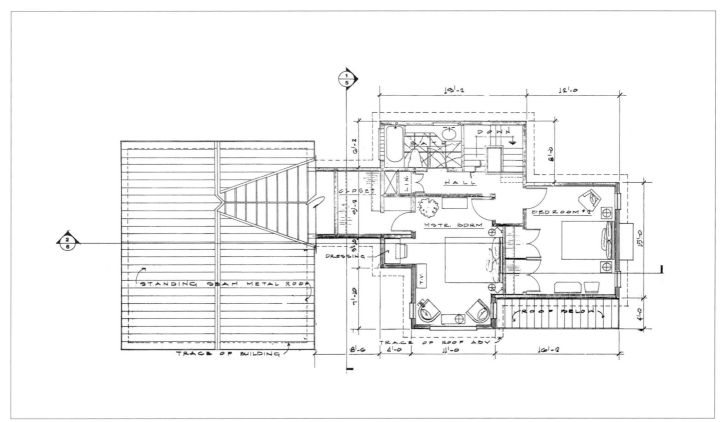

Second Floor Plan

North Elevation

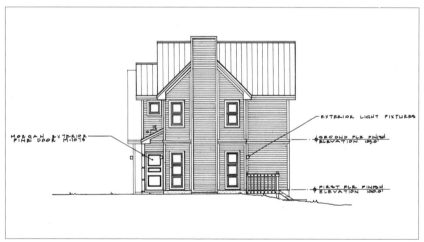

South Elevation

East Elevation

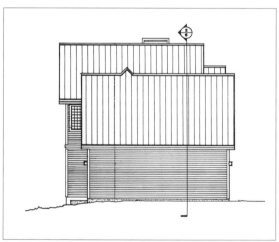

West Elevation

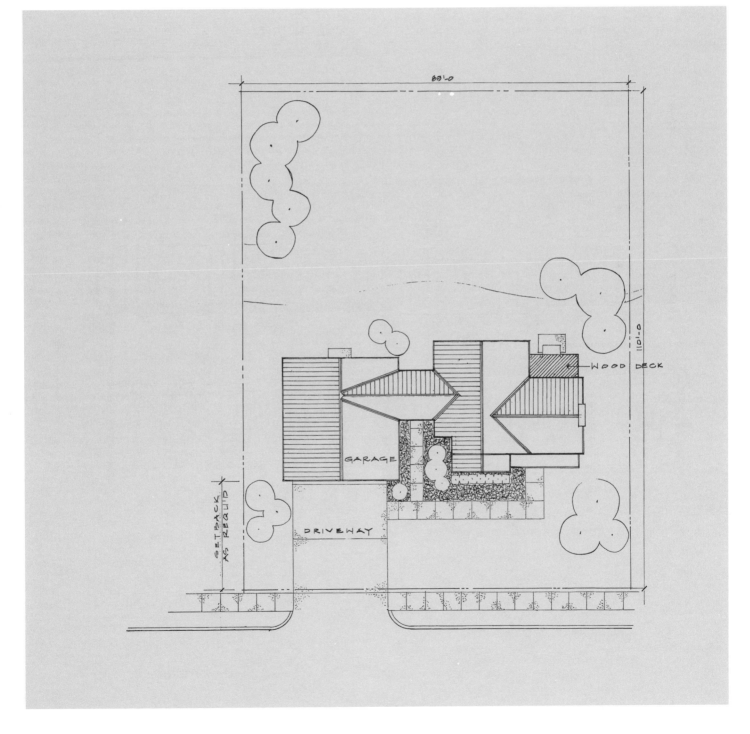

Section A-A

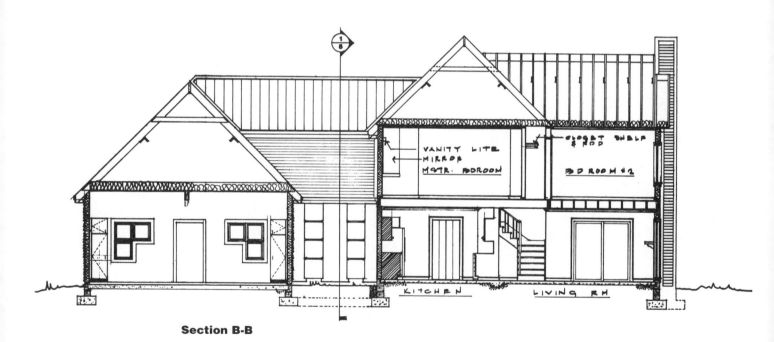

Section B-B

Wall Section

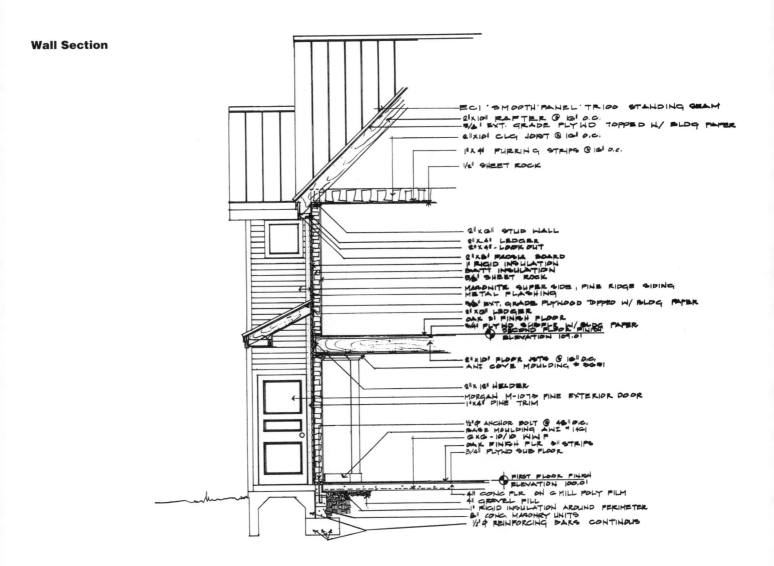

ECI 'SMOOTH' PANEL TR100 STANDING SEAM
2"x10" RAFTER @ 16" O.C.
5/8" EXT. GRADE PLYWD TOPPED W/ BLDG PAPER
2"x10" CLG JOIST @ 16" O.C.

1"x4" FURRING STRIPS @ 16" O.C.

1/2" SHEET ROCK

2"x8" STUD WALL
2"x4" LEDGER
2"x4" LOOK OUT
2"x8" FASCIA BOARD
1" RIGID INSULATION
BATT INSULATION
5/8" SHEET ROCK
MASONITE SUPER SIDE, PINE RIDGE SIDING
METAL FLASHING
5/8" EXT. GRADE PLYWOOD TOPPED W/ BLDG PAPER
2"x8" LEDGER
OAK 3" FINISH FLOOR
3/4" PLYWD SUBFLOOR W/ BLDG PAPER
SECOND FLOOR FINISH
ELEVATION 109.01

2"x10" FLOOR JOISTS @ 16" O.C.
ANT COVE MOULDING # 5651

2"x12" HEADER
MORGAN M-1075 PINE EXTERIOR DOOR
1"x4" PINE TRIM

1/2" Ø ANCHOR BOLT @ 48" O.C.
BASE MOULDING AWI #1461
6x6 - 10/10 WWF
OAK FINISH FLR 3" STRIPS
3/4" PLYWD SUB FLOOR

FIRST FLOOR FINISH
ELEVATION 100.01
4" CONC FLR ON 6 MILL POLY FILM
4" GRAVEL FILL
1" RIGID INSULATION AROUND PERIMETER
8" CONC. MASONRY UNITS
1/2" Ø REINFORCING BARS CONTINUOUS

Perspective

DiCicco

A clever floor plan. The sawtooth perimeter makes the courtyards a vital part of the house. Well suited for a desert site or small suburban lot.
DON METZ

Stepbacks are used to maximize exposure. Great sense of openness, yet roof overhang gives good protection. Elevations need work.
PETER WOERNER

David B. DiCicco

Designed for the Sonoran Desert, this home responds to the rigorously hot climate and a leftover, oddly shaped building site. The combination of sun and site helped suggest the stepped three-module plan and large-angled, sun-shading roof. Stepping and nesting the 24-foot-square modules to follow the southeast lot line afforded the opportunity to continuously open the cooler northeast side to the outdoors. The sun shade roof floats protectively over the living modules for maximum ventilation and covering for the HVAC and DWH equipment. Its angled shape yields huge effective overhangs to protect wall areas and also helps direct the eye along a longer, more dynamic line. In addition to the sun shade, desert-tolerant trees are planted around the west, southwest, south, and east sides of the house to protectively shade walls and cool the adjacent ground.

Space within the home is visually maximized by allowing the viewer to look diagonally across and through the space . . . usually directly to the outside. A single floor material, colored and patterned concrete, flows from inside to out, enhancing the feeling of spaciousness. Nine-foot-high ceilings and continuous clerestory windows allow natural light without sun to further connect the occupant with the outside.

David B. DiCicco

TECHNICAL DATA

Gross Square Feet:
1,248

Location:
Phoenix, Arizona

Materials and Construction:

FOUNDATION AND FLOOR:
Concrete

WALLS:
Masonry load bearing and post and beam; rock-faced concrete masonry units are turned inside to provide a warm hue

ROOF:
Heavy timber wood trusses with metal roofing

Estimated Cost to Build:
$60,000

Estimated Heating/ Cooling Costs:
$700

Site Plan

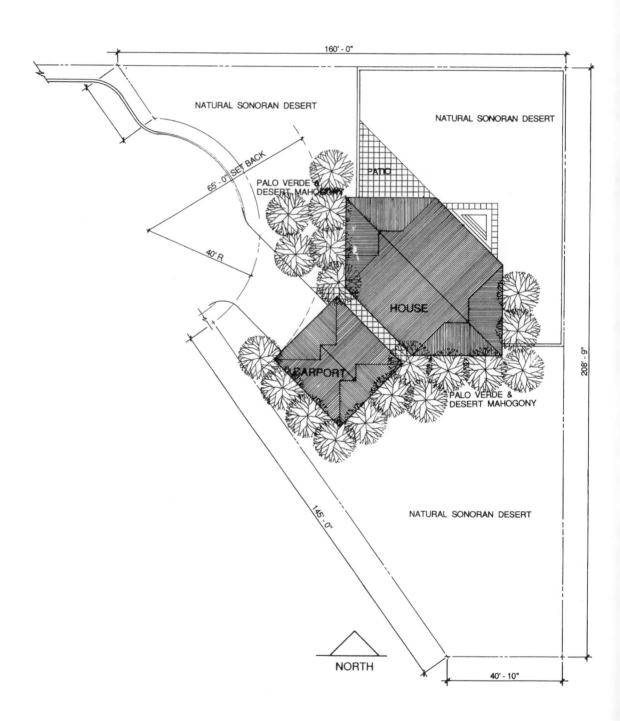

160' - 0"

NATURAL SONORAN DESERT

NATURAL SONORAN DESERT

65' - 0" SET BACK

PALO VERDE &
DESERT MAHOGONY

PATIO

40' R

HOUSE

208' - 9"

CARPORT

PALO VERDE &
DESERT MAHOGONY

145 - 0"

NATURAL SONORAN DESERT

NORTH

40' - 10"

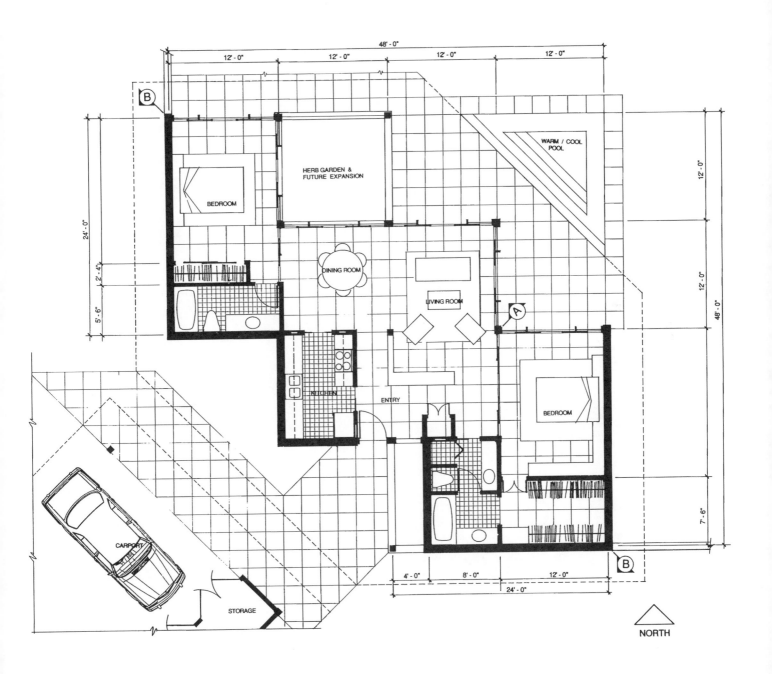

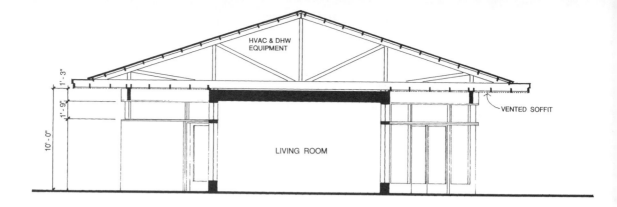

Cross Section

HVAC & DHW EQUIPMENT

VENTED SOFFIT

1' - 3"

1' - 9"

10' - 0"

LIVING ROOM

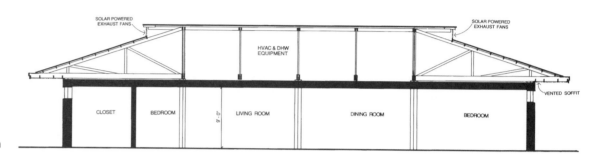

Longitudinal Section

SOLAR POWERED EXHAUST FANS

SOLAR POWERED EXHAUST FANS

HVAC & DHW EQUIPMENT

VENTED SOFFIT

CLOSET | BEDROOM | LIVING ROOM | DINING ROOM | BEDROOM

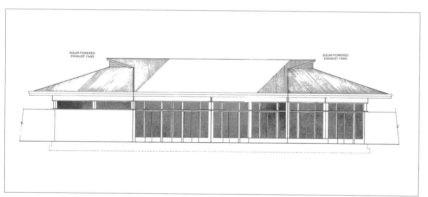

Northeast Elevation

SOLAR POWERED EXHAUST FANS

SOLAR POWERED EXHAUST FANS

Northwest Elevation

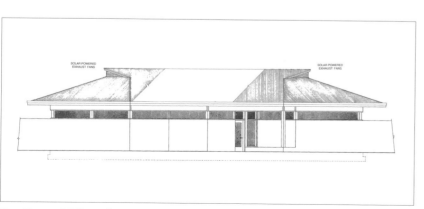

Southwest Elevation

SOLAR POWERED EXHAUST FANS

SOLAR POWERED EXHAUST FANS

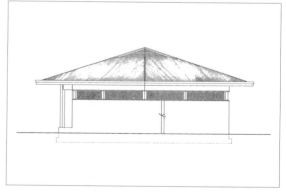

Southeast Elevation

Wall Section

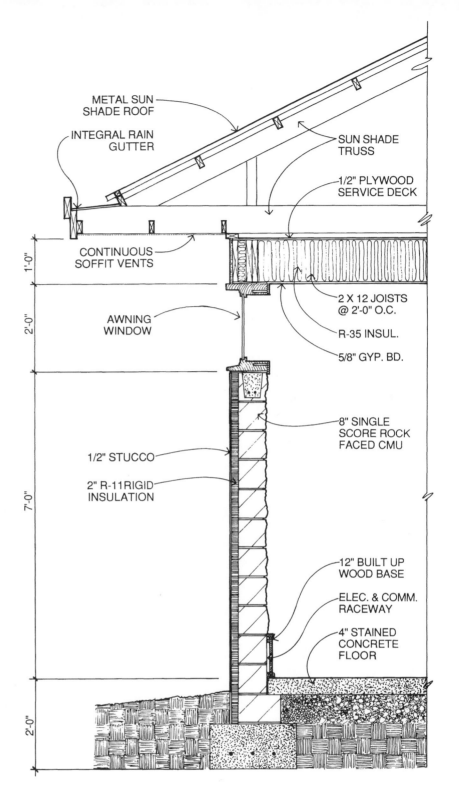

METAL SUN SHADE ROOF

INTEGRAL RAIN GUTTER

SUN SHADE TRUSS

1/2" PLYWOOD SERVICE DECK

CONTINUOUS SOFFIT VENTS

2 X 12 JOISTS @ 2'-0" O.C.

R-35 INSUL.

5/8" GYP. BD.

AWNING WINDOW

8" SINGLE SCORE ROCK FACED CMU

1/2" STUCCO

2" R-11 RIGID INSULATION

12" BUILT UP WOOD BASE

ELEC. & COMM. RACEWAY

4" STAINED CONCRETE FLOOR

1'-0"

2'-0"

7'-0"

2'-0"

Perspective

The Riverton Residence

Area of Lot: 16,200 sq. ft.
Area of House: 1,200 sq. ft.

Fritschij

All the economies of the basic "ranch house," with an open and efficient plan.
DON METZ

Stretched-out linear plan. Simple, open. An unpretentious house.
PETER WOERNER

Michael J. Fritschij

This home is designed for a retiring couple with a love for the outdoors in both winter and summer. The home's formal front, verandah, and entry court address the vernacular architecture in the surrounding community. Extensive natural landscaping provides privacy from the street to the sun deck and patio. The house then acts as a gateway, opening up to spectacular views to the south. The verandah's design allows for it to be enclosed, extending its use into both the spring and autumn seasons.

In the interior, the wood stove acts as the central focus for the living area and country kitchen.

Through the arrangement of furnishings, the open plan creates a casual atmosphere with the possibility for both large or smaller, more intimate gatherings taking place. As a space-saving measure, the bathroom serves as both a guest powder room and an ensuite for the master bedroom. The extensive use of glazing on the south facade allows winter sun to penetrate the home and summer breezes off the lake to filter through the house, cooling it. The home is planned on a single level, allowing for the mobility of residents in later years.

Michael J. Fritschij

TECHNICAL DATA

Gross Square Feet:
1,200

Location:
Riverton, Manitoba, Canada, on the shores of Lake Winnipeg

Materials:
Wood framing; concrete grade beam foundation; superinsulated for added energy savings; exterior cladding — painted wood siding; gypsum wallboard interior; hardwood flooring in living area

Type:
Wood frame

Estimated Cost to Build:
$53,000 (Canadian)

Estimated Heating/Cooling Costs:
$448 (Canadian)

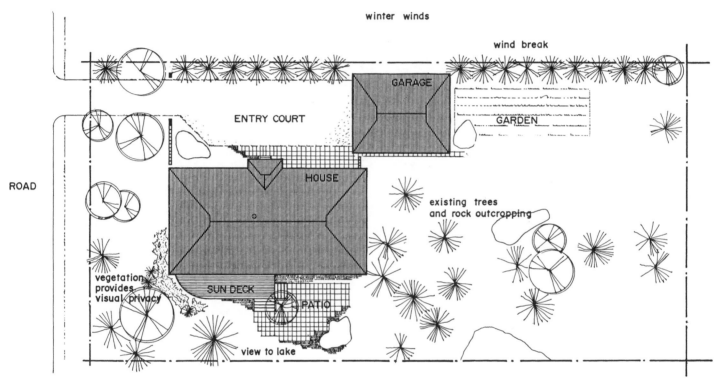

ROAD

winter winds

wind break

GARAGE

ENTRY COURT

GARDEN

HOUSE

existing trees
and rock outcropping

vegetation
provides
visual privacy

SUN DECK

PATIO

view to lake

summer breeze off lake

Floor Plan

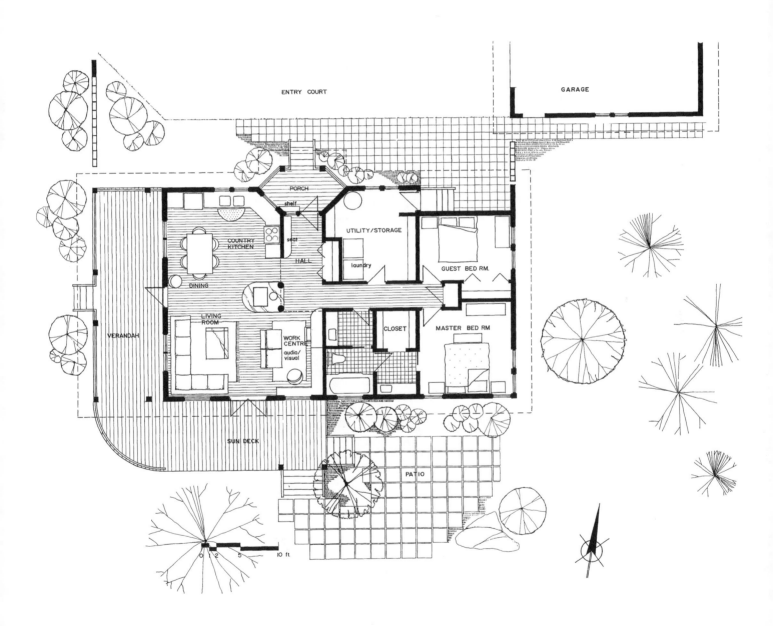

ENTRY COURT

GARAGE

PORCH

shelf

UTILITY/STORAGE

COUNTRY KITCHEN

seat

laundry

GUEST BED RM.

HALL

DINING

LIVING ROOM

WORK CENTRE

audio/visual

CLOSET

MASTER BED RM

VERANDAH

SUN DECK

PATIO

0 2 5   10 ft.

East Elevation

West Elevation

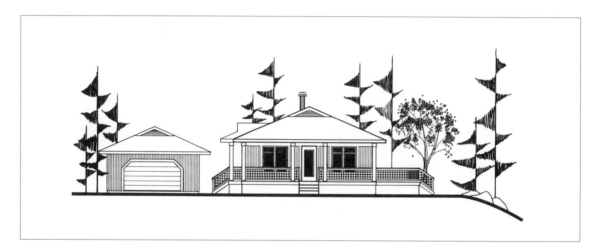

North Elevation

South Elevation

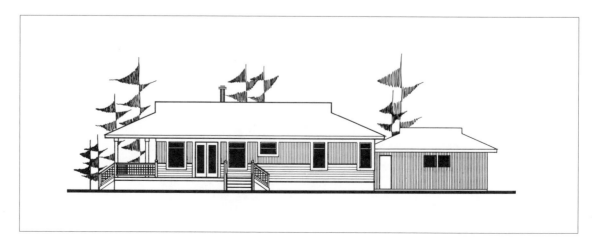

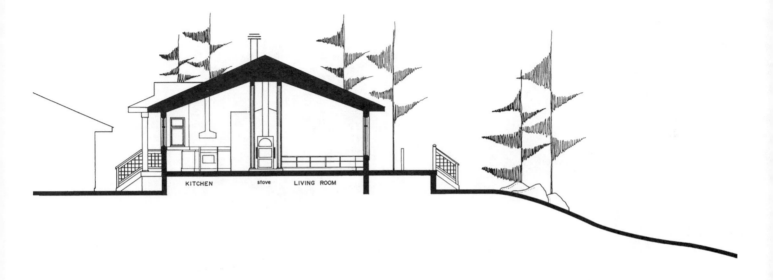

KITCHEN   stove   LIVING ROOM

Perspective

Grandy

Exciting, wild plan. Spatially exciting. A demanding house — costly. Don't build or general contract yourself unless you've been around at least once.
PETER WOERNER

A challenging environment, a piece of live-in sculpture. Interesting combination of forms and spaces both coming apart and hanging together.
DON METZ

Daniel Grandy

The primary issue addressed in this compact house is that of "wall" and how it is sensitive to site and environmental conditions. The site is a coastal point which has a fair climate and tropical breezes throughout most of the year. The possibility of extremely turbulent storms is, however, a concern.

The waterfront location brings to us images of sea-going vessels from distant ports and pleasure boats enjoying a calm afternoon. These contrasting images of "vessel" and "boat" help establish a dichotomy of function and form: a vessel is an independent, enduring, and enclosed instrument; a pleasure boat is restricted, vulnerable, and open.

These same images are expressed in the "house-vessel" on the north, which is rigid against harsh winds and stands tall to separate public from private domains. In contrast, the "house-boat" on the south

is passive in form and solar qualities, expressed through the south glazing being echoed by the exploding out of the frame — a metaphor of its vulnerability.

The "wall" strengthens and reiterates this dichotomy of form through relationships of solid/void (the breakdown of the east facade), presence/absence (the presence of glass in the absence of the solid vessel on the north), and enclosure/extension (the battening of tarpaulins to the space frame in times of bad weather, directly conflicting with its movement away from the south glazing).

In retrospect: ideally, a house that's ready to sail; in reality, a summer home that mirrors its surroundings.

Daniel Grandy

TECHNICAL DATA

Gross Square Feet:
1,250

Location:
Coastal; moderate climate

Materials:
Concrete foundation and floor slab; heavy timber and steel space frame structure; wood and plaster on light timber in-fill; metal sheet on steel space frame; glass curtain wall; rubber membrane roofing

Type:
Post and beam (heavy timber and steel); steel space frame

Estimated Cost to Build:
N/A

Estimated Heating/ Cooling Costs:
N/A

Site Plan

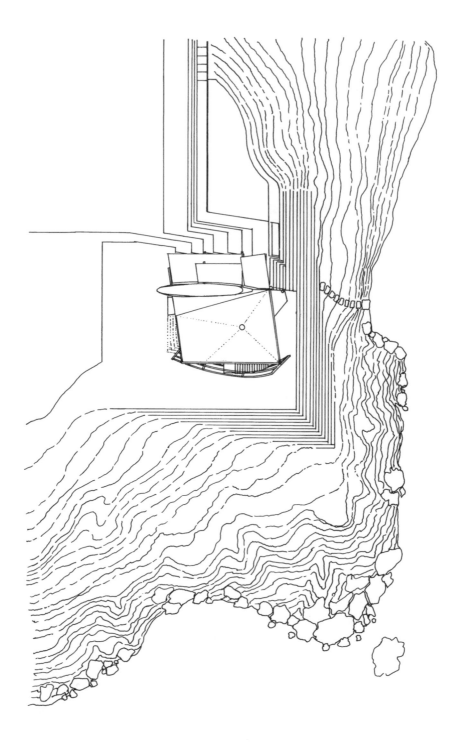

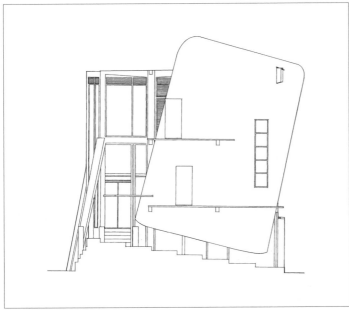

North Elevation

East Elevation

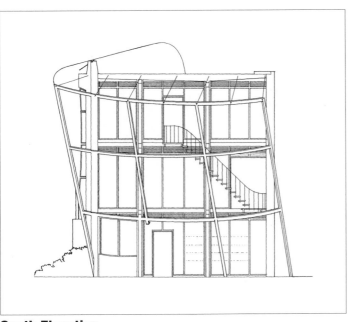

South Elevation

West Elevation

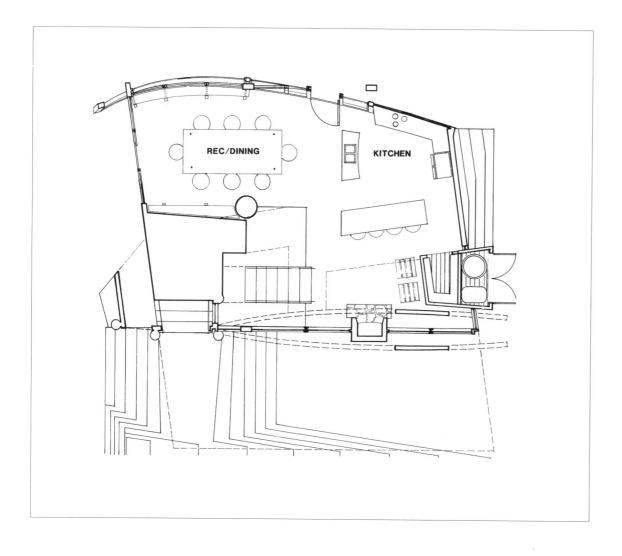

REC/DINING

KITCHEN

Second Floor Plan

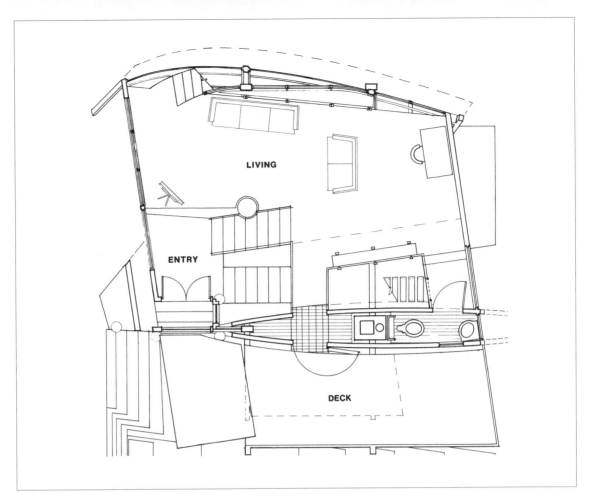

Third Floor Plan

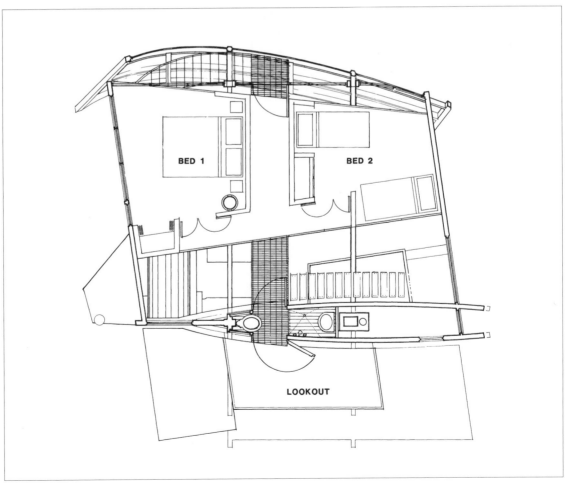

Section

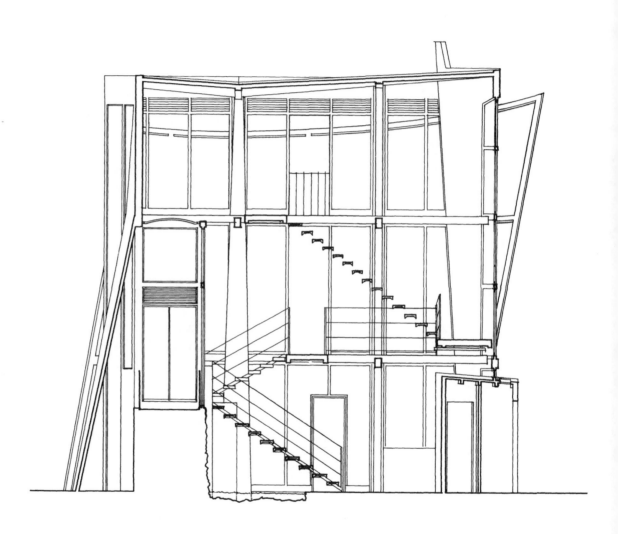

South Wall Section

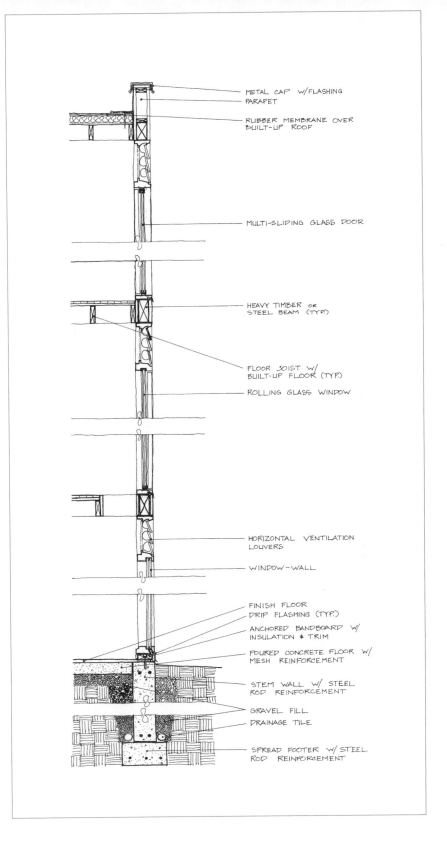

METAL CAP W/FLASHING
PARAPET

RUBBER MEMBRANE OVER
BUILT-UP ROOF

MULTI-SLIDING GLASS DOOR

HEAVY TIMBER OR
STEEL BEAM (TYP.)

FLOOR JOIST W/
BUILT-UP FLOOR (TYP.)

ROLLING GLASS WINDOW

HORIZONTAL VENTILATION
LOUVERS

WINDOW-WALL

FINISH FLOOR
DRIP FLASHING (TYP.)

ANCHORED BANDBOARD W/
INSULATION & TRIM

POURED CONCRETE FLOOR W/
MESH REINFORCEMENT

STEM WALL W/ STEEL
ROD REINFORCEMENT

GRAVEL FILL
DRAINAGE TILE

SPREAD FOOTER W/ STEEL
ROD REINFORCEMENT

Perspective (Axonometric)

92

Harris

JURY COMMENTS

A six-square plan on two floors with lots of vertical space above the living area. Landscaping is critical in "placing" the house.
DON METZ

Nice height in section. Good sense of movement to exterior.
PETER WOERNER

David A. Harris

The house is organized on a stacked nominal 12'x12'x10' nine-square grid. The architectural style and materials are indigenous to the coastal Northwest: expressive but simple forms and geometry, elements of whimsy, and openness to relieve "cabin fever" and increase natural light and a feeling of warmth in frequently overcast skies.

The central south-facing solarium/entry and spiral stair is the organizational and visual focal point of the plan and volume and provides a serving area for entertaining. The upper glazing continues second-floor views to the south via louvered doors and frames to Goat Mountain and the National Forest and maximizes solar gain in winter. The side windows are placed for cross-ventilation and intimate views of landscape elements. Bedrooms on the second level have private decks, which also have southerly views and exposure. Corner forms house stove flues and create supports for light globes and pennants.

David A. Harris

TECHNICAL DATA

Gross Square Feet:
1,238 (excluding decks)

Location:
Bayview, Lake Pend
O'Reille, Idaho

Materials:
Painted redwood siding/
decking; low-E glazing;
metal and single-ply
membrane roofing

Type:
Wood frame

**Estimated Cost
to Build:**
$65,000

**Estimated Heating/
Cooling Costs:**
$300 per season

*Production assistance by
Tom Theisen*

*Interior design by
Patsy O'Connor*

Site Plan

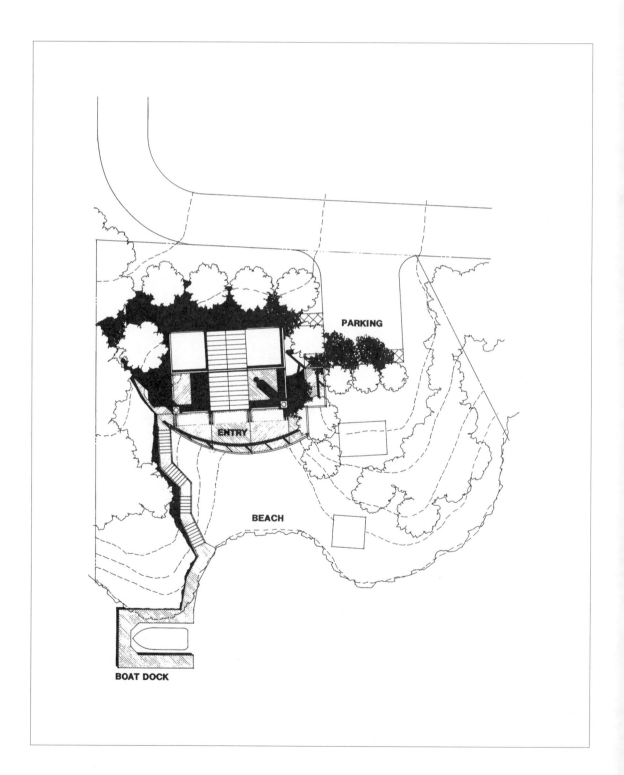

PARKING

ENTRY

BEACH

BOAT DOCK

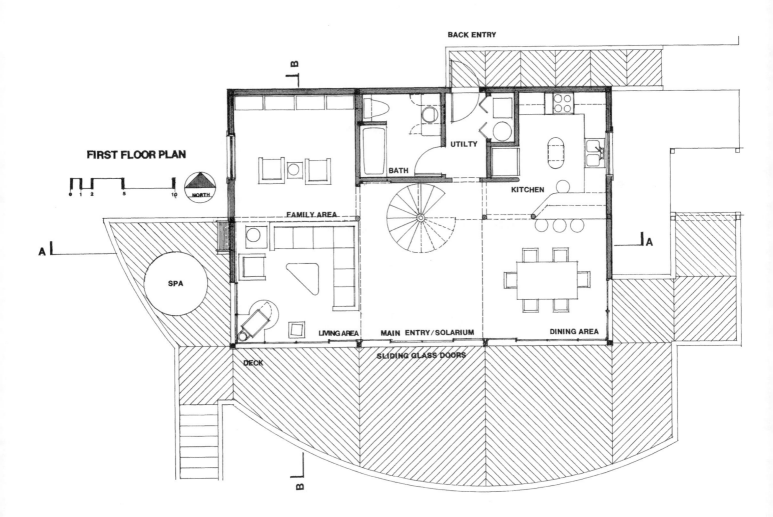

FIRST FLOOR PLAN

NORTH

0 1 2   5   10

BACK ENTRY

B

UTILTY

BATH

A

KITCHEN

FAMILY AREA

SPA

A

LIVING AREA   MAIN ENTRY/SOLARIUM   DINING AREA

DECK   SLIDING GLASS DOORS

B

95

Second Floor Plan

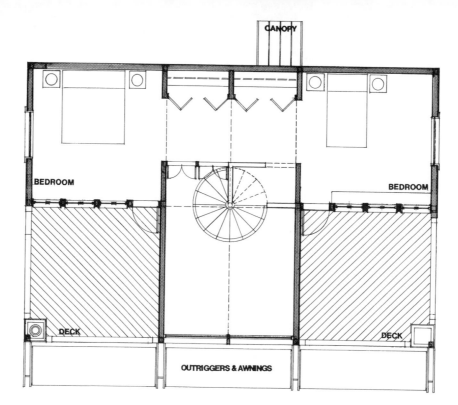

CANOPY

BEDROOM

BEDROOM

DECK

DECK

OUTRIGGERS & AWNINGS

**Alternate Second
Floor Plan**

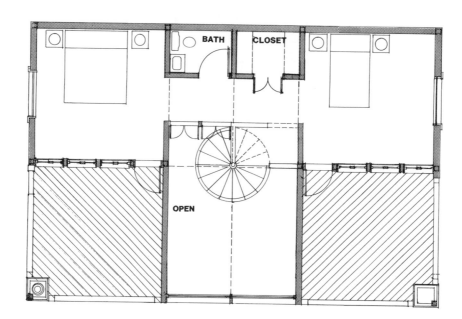

BATH

CLOSET

OPEN

96

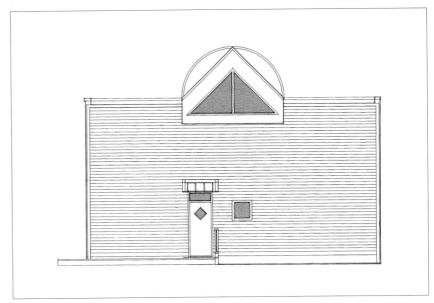

North Elevation

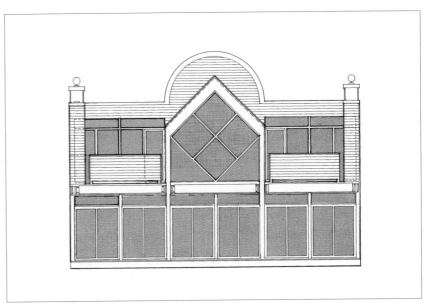

South Elevation

AWNING

East Elevation

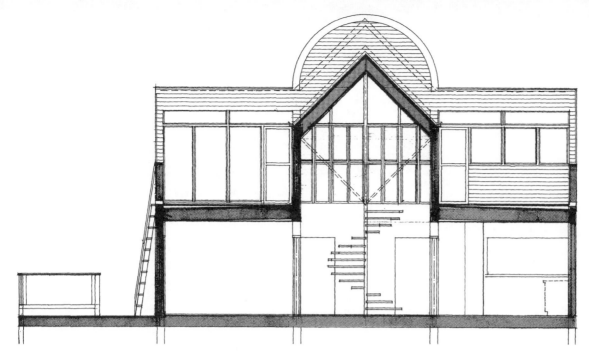

Section A-A

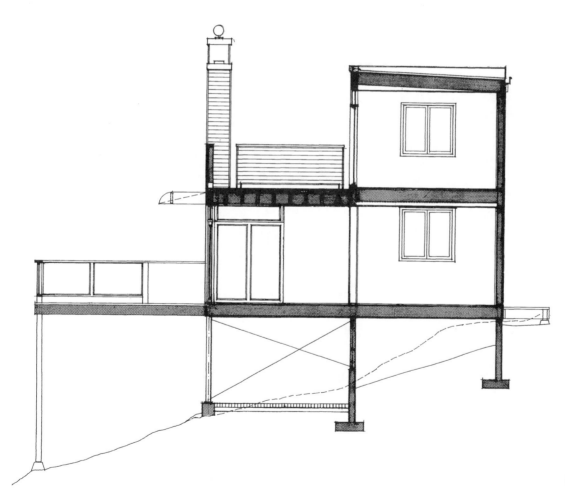

Section B-B

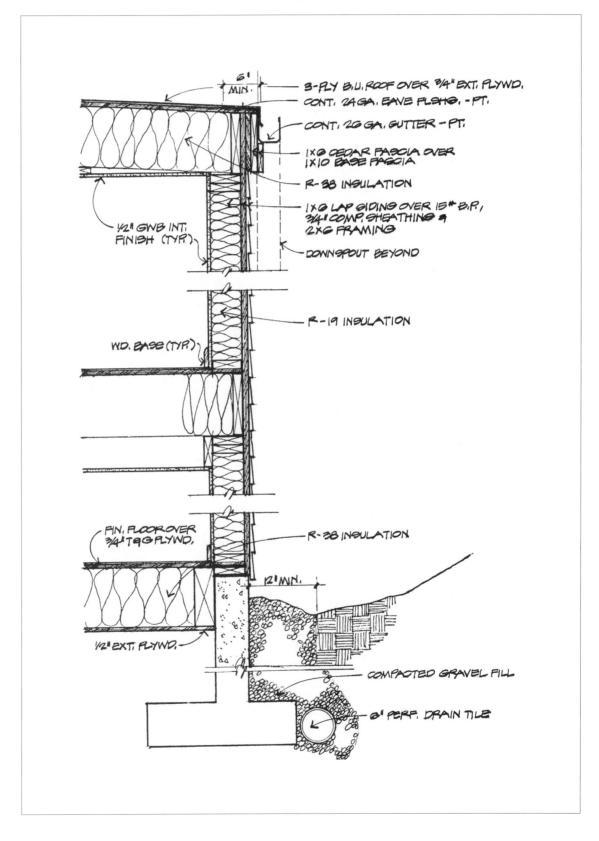

3-PLY B.U. ROOF OVER ¾" EXT. PLYWD.

CONT. 24 GA. EAVE FLSHG. - PT.

CONT. 26 GA. GUTTER - PT.

1X6 CEDAR FASCIA OVER
1X10 BASE FASCIA

R-38 INSULATION

1X6 LAP SIDING OVER 15# B.P.,
¾" COMP. SHEATHING &
2X6 FRAMING

DOWNSPOUT BEYOND

R-19 INSULATION

6'
MIN.

½" GWB INT.
FINISH (TYP.)

W.D. BASE (TYP.)

FIN. FLOOR OVER
¾" T&G PLYWD.

R-38 INSULATION

12" MIN.

½" EXT. PLYWD.

COMPACTED GRAVEL FILL

6" PERF. DRAIN TILE

Perspective

Haskell

JURY COMMENTS

Clean derivative forms. Sturdy presence. Offers good possibilities for expansion. Would be perfect in a grove of tall trees.
DON METZ

Nice Victorian barn — simple gable.
PETER WOERNER

Thomas McClellan Haskell

Although suitable for most regions of the United States, this house design is reminiscent of the farmhouses and barns which dot the New England countryside. A cruciform plan clusters functions around a compact service core. Rooms are clearly defined while maintaining a sense of spatial continuity. Circulation square footage is minimized. Living areas extend outside to trellised porches. An unfinished basement provides convenient expansion opportunities.

Windows are located to catch southern sun and promote cross-ventilation. A cupola introduces daylight to the center of the house. East and west facades are windowless to ensure privacy from neighboring dwellings or to facilitate connection as a multiple unit structure (with minor modification).

Thomas McClellan Haskell

TECHNICAL DATA

Gross Square Feet:
1,136

Materials:
Concrete footings and foundations; wood framing, batt insulation; insulated sheathing; natural finish vertical redwood siding with painted wood trim; fiberglass shingles; wood doors; prefinished window units; gypsum board with painted wood trim; hardwood flooring; carpeting; ceramic tile

Mechanical System:
High-efficiency pulse furnace, forced hot air

Estimated Cost to Build:
1,136 sq. ft. @ $125.00/sq. ft. = 142,000

Estimated Heating/ Cooling Costs:
$1,022 ($0.90/sq. ft.) per year

Site Plan

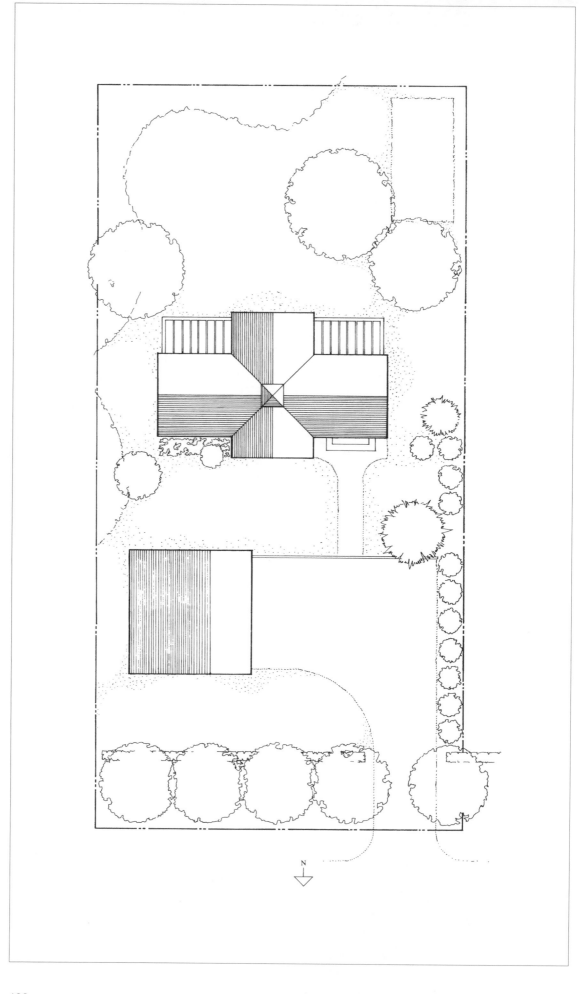

North Elevation

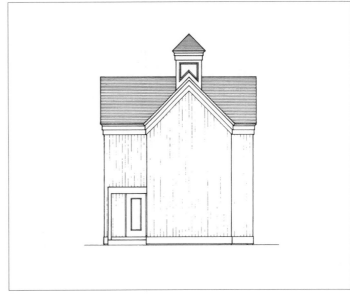

East Elevation

South Elevation

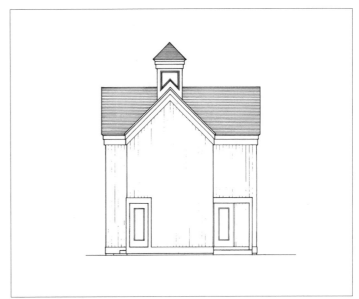

West Elevation

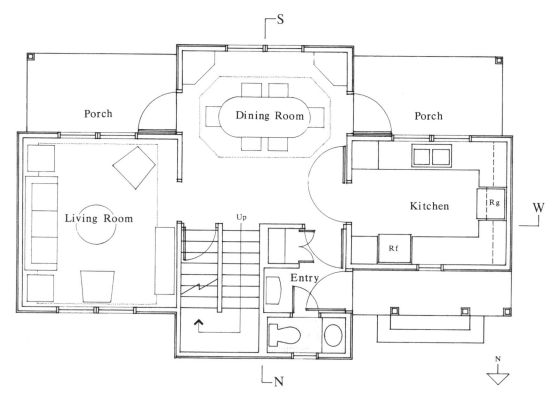

First Floor Plan

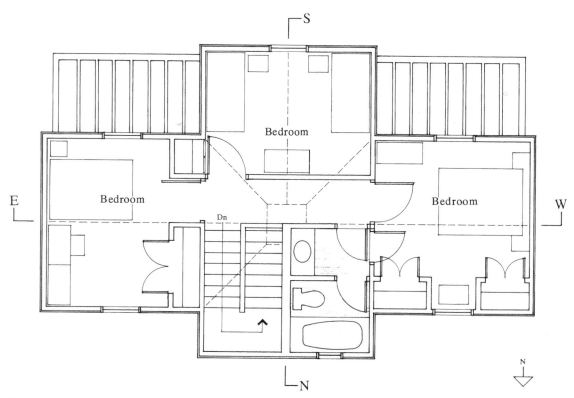

Second Floor Plan

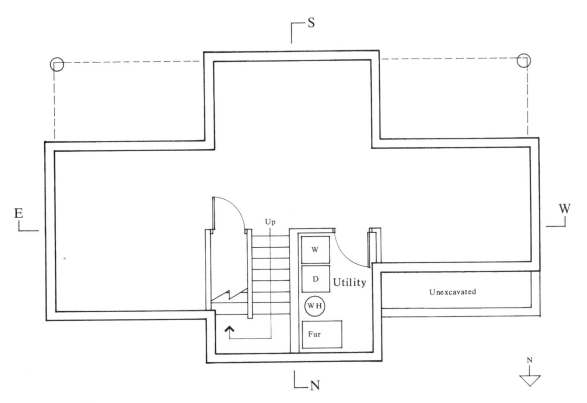

Basement Plan

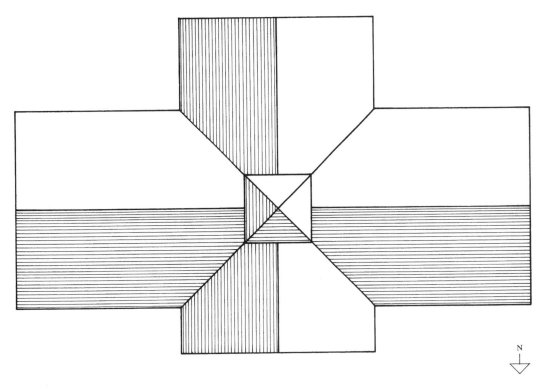

Roof Plan

105

E-W Section

2nd Flr

1st Flr

Bsmt

8'-0"

8'-10"

8'-10"

N-S Section

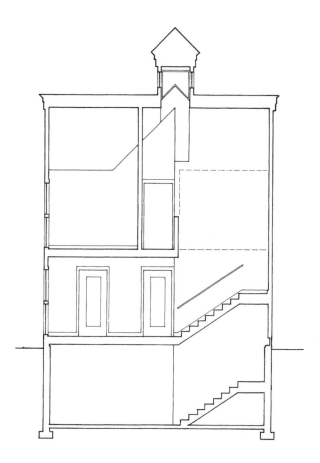

106

Wall Section

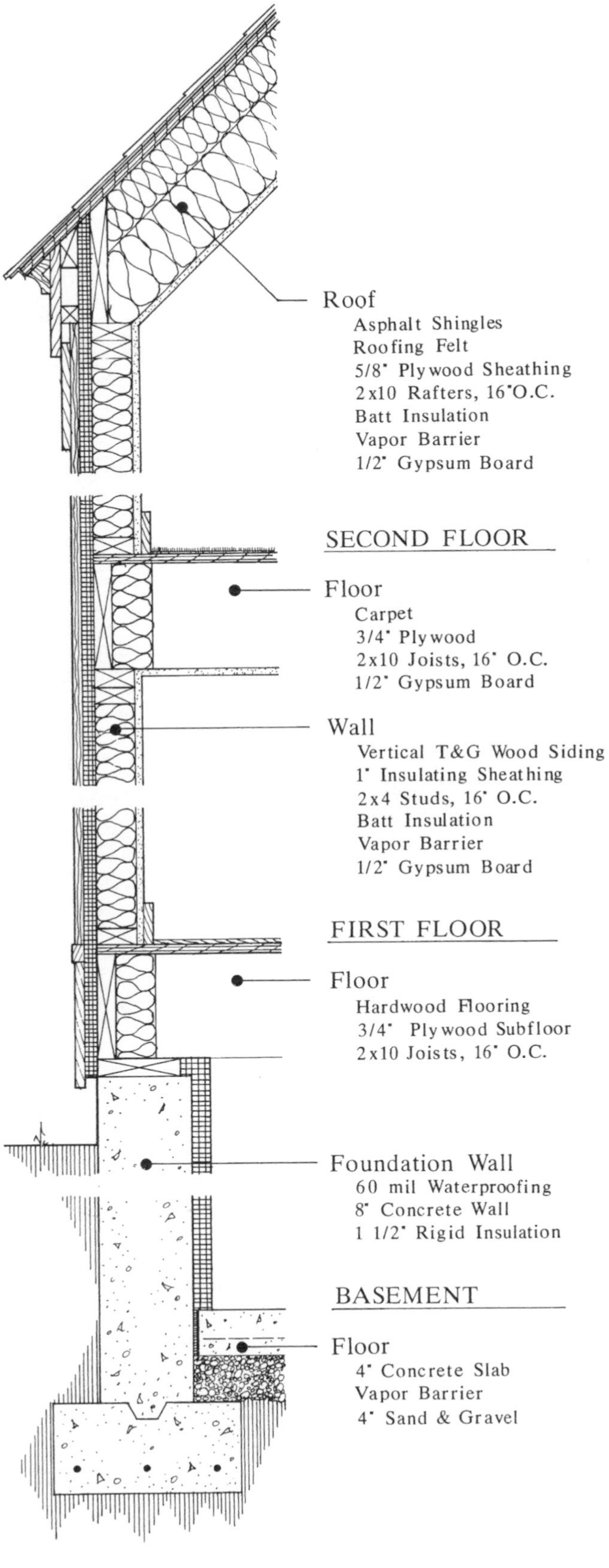

Roof
- Asphalt Shingles
- Roofing Felt
- 5/8" Plywood Sheathing
- 2x10 Rafters, 16"O.C.
- Batt Insulation
- Vapor Barrier
- 1/2" Gypsum Board

SECOND FLOOR

Floor
- Carpet
- 3/4" Plywood
- 2x10 Joists, 16" O.C.
- 1/2" Gypsum Board

Wall
- Vertical T&G Wood Siding
- 1" Insulating Sheathing
- 2x4 Studs, 16" O.C.
- Batt Insulation
- Vapor Barrier
- 1/2" Gypsum Board

FIRST FLOOR

Floor
- Hardwood Flooring
- 3/4" Plywood Subfloor
- 2x10 Joists, 16" O.C.

Foundation Wall
- 60 mil Waterproofing
- 8" Concrete Wall
- 1 1/2" Rigid Insulation

BASEMENT

Floor
- 4" Concrete Slab
- Vapor Barrier
- 4" Sand & Gravel

Perspective

Huber

Classic rural style. Informal, easy-going architecture. Inexpensive to build and maintain.
DON METZ

Dining room and living room compound. A nice large space.
PETER WOERNER

J. Whitney Huber

RIVER HOUSE

This house was designed as a retirement home for a couple with married children and grandchildren who would be occasional visitors. They wanted a practical, small house that would provide them with all their living on one floor, would locate the guest quarters apart from their bedroom, and would be economical to heat and cool. Their property had sweeping views over a tidal marsh toward the mouth of the Connecticut River. They wanted their house to take advantage of the views and to have a character befitting the waterside setting.

The house is composed of a compact, two-level block of bedrooms and baths attached to a comparatively voluminous living/dining/kitchen room. The house entry is a contained, low-ceilinged space that opens to the upward and outward expansion of the living space – the effect is to diminish the feeling of smallness in the compact spaces of the house. The supporting truss spanning the living space implies a separation of living and dining spaces within the large room. The fireplace is a major focus of the living space that encourages a grouping of furniture around it. The exterior massing and detailing of the house has its roots in the Shingle-style beach cottages that are part of the history of this area of the Connecticut coast.

The house in its first winter was economical to heat and performed well as a passive solar design. During the coldest winter month, the fuel oil bill was $94.00 (1990 cost). Sea breezes from Long Island Sound keep the house deliciously cool on the hottest of summer days.

J. Whitney Huber

TECHNICAL DATA

Gross Square Feet:
1,250

Location:
Upland site near the mouth of the Connecticut River

Materials:
Wood shingle exterior; asphalt shingle roof; wood casement windows with insulating glass; gypsum board interior walls and ceilings; hardwood floors in living spaces

Type:
Stick-built on concrete foundation

Mechanical Systems:
Oil-fired forced hot air heating system; private well and septic system

Estimated Cost to Build:
$155,000

Estimated Heating/ Cooling Costs:
Less than $600 per year

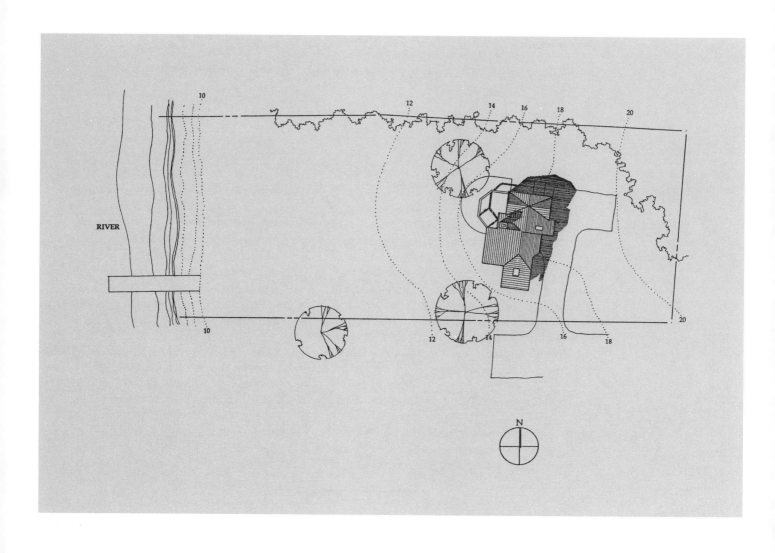

RIVER

10

12

14

16

18

20

10

12

14

16

18

20

N

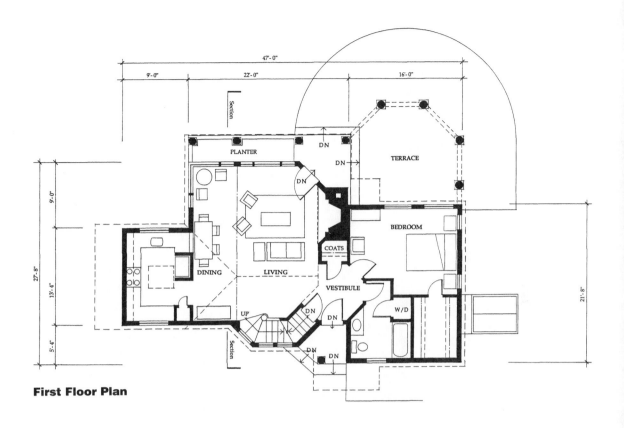

First Floor Plan

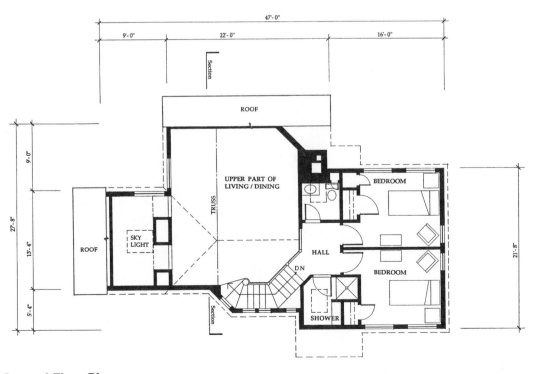

Second Floor Plan

Axonometric

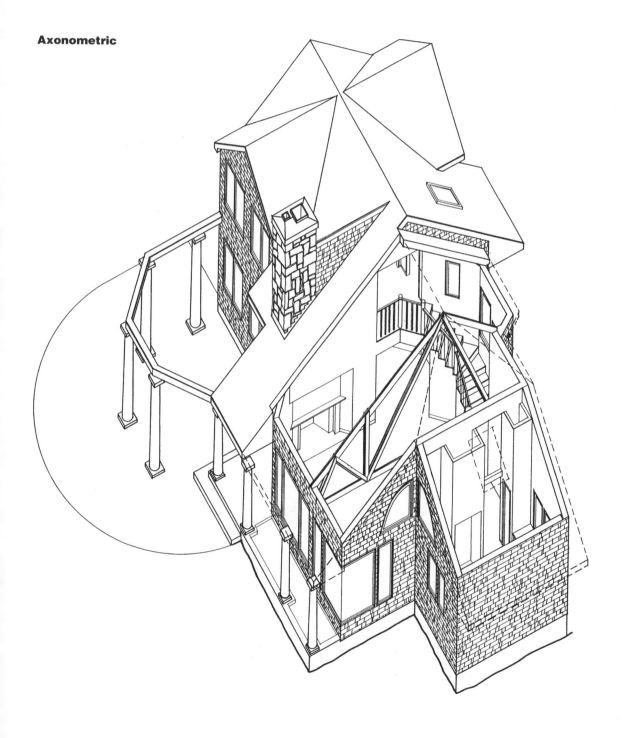

East Elevation

RIDGE

14'-7 3/4"

2 ND

8'-5 3/4"

1 ST

West Elevation

North Elevation

South Elevation

113

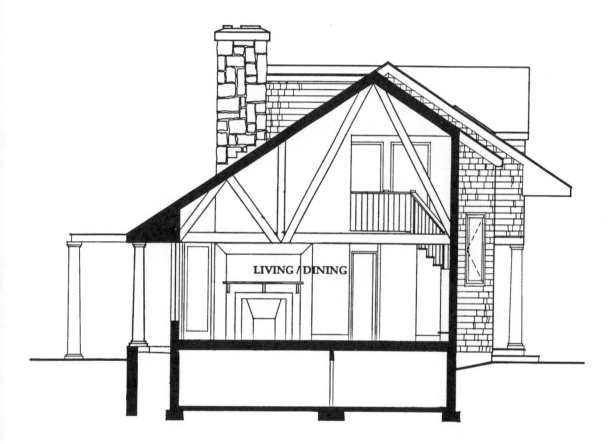

LIVING / DINING

Wall Section

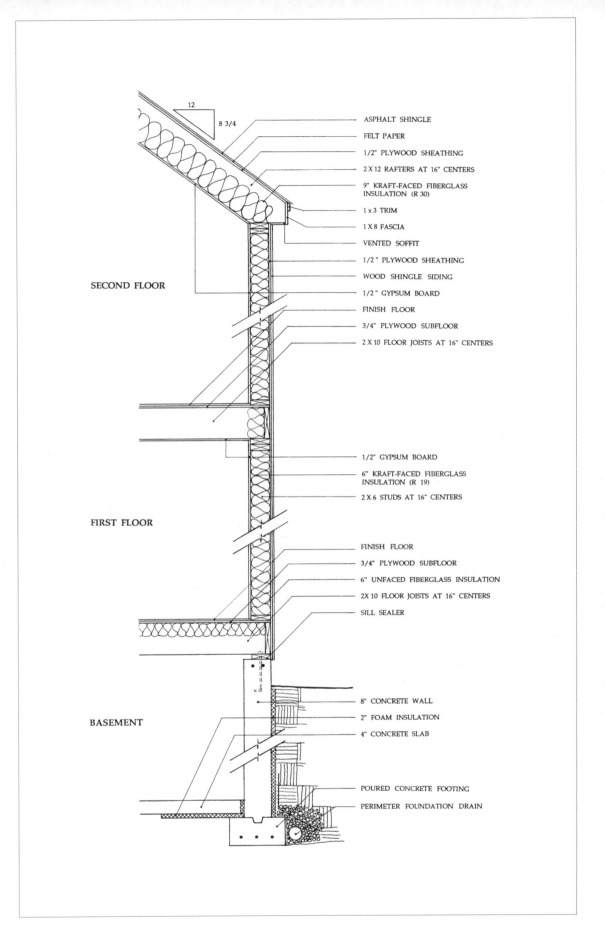

12
8 3/4

SECOND FLOOR

FIRST FLOOR

BASEMENT

ASPHALT SHINGLE
FELT PAPER
1/2" PLYWOOD SHEATHING
2 X 12 RAFTERS AT 16" CENTERS
9" KRAFT-FACED FIBERGLASS INSULATION (R 30)
1 x 3 TRIM
1 X 8 FASCIA
VENTED SOFFIT
1/2 " PLYWOOD SHEATHING
WOOD SHINGLE SIDING
1/2 " GYPSUM BOARD
FINISH FLOOR
3/4" PLYWOOD SUBFLOOR
2 X 10 FLOOR JOISTS AT 16" CENTERS

1/2" GYPSUM BOARD
6" KRAFT-FACED FIBERGLASS INSULATION (R 19)
2 X 6 STUDS AT 16" CENTERS

FINISH FLOOR
3/4" PLYWOOD SUBFLOOR
6" UNFACED FIBERGLASS INSULATION
2X 10 FLOOR JOISTS AT 16" CENTERS
SILL SEALER

8" CONCRETE WALL
2" FOAM INSULATION
4" CONCRETE SLAB

POURED CONCRETE FOOTING
PERIMETER FOUNDATION DRAIN

115

Perspective

Huber

Simple, ordered facade. Strong, durable axis. Simple massing with wings.
PETER WOERNER

Cute little Shingle-style house with lots of personality and room. Nice juxtaposition of the long and the narrow facades.
DON METZ

NARROW HOUSE

J. Whitney Huber

This house was designed for a young couple with a child on a limited income as their "starter home." They wanted a distinctive house that was economical to build. They also wished to have a passive solar-heated house that could be supplemented with wood heat. The house was designed with an electric backup heating system.

The main body of the house has a finished interior dimension of 12 feet by 36 feet. The ground floor is a single room for living, with a minimal division of the kitchen and the dining room. The wood stove, its hearth, and flanking decorative columns make a subtle separation of living and dining spaces. Upstairs, two bedrooms abut a centrally located bath and laundry. Above the bath, in the peak of the house, is a garretlike loft. The narrow east end of the house with its sidewinder porch is the "front" of the house. The long south wall is amply glazed to provide solar gain in the winter months. In the summer months, the surrounding trees shade the south wall.

The house has performed very well for the couple. Heating costs have been low. Natural ventilation keeps the house cool in the summer. The open plan on the first floor has given them a great amount of flexibility in their living space. The upstairs arrangement of end bedrooms with good light and ventilation and the central bath and laundry is an efficient layout that provides maximum privacy. The loft above the bath is a good workspace and provides guest sleeping quarters when needed.

J. Whitney Huber

TECHNICAL DATA

Gross Square Feet:
1,150 (excluding porches and outside storage)

Location:
Wooded site in coastal Connecticut

Materials:
Wood clapboard exterior; asphalt shingle roof; wood sliding windows with insulating glass; gypsum board interior walls and ceilings; pine and ceramic tile floors in living spaces

Type:
Stick-built on masonry foundation

Mechanical Systems:
Wood heat with backup electric heating; private well and septic system

Estimated Cost to Build:
$95,000

Estimated Heating/ Cooling Costs:
Less than $500

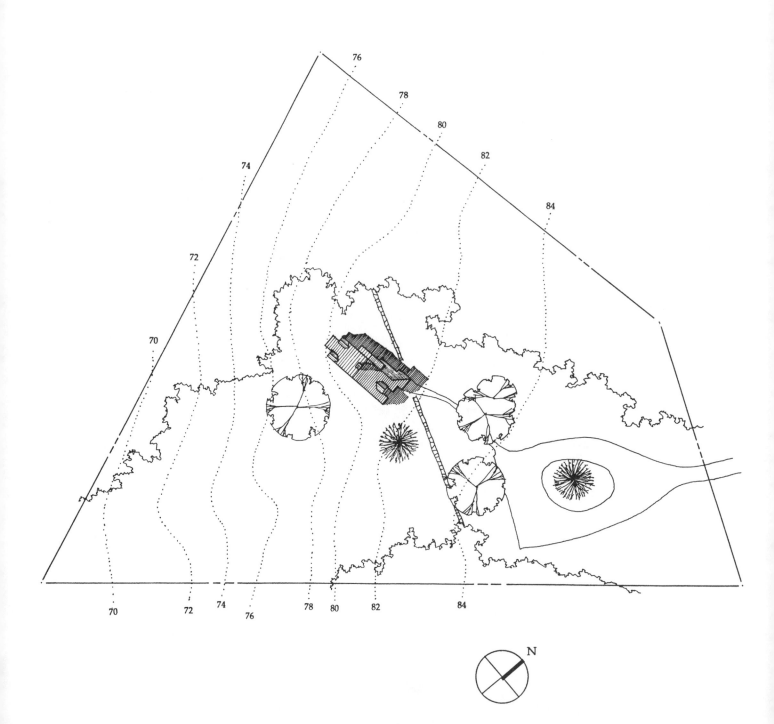

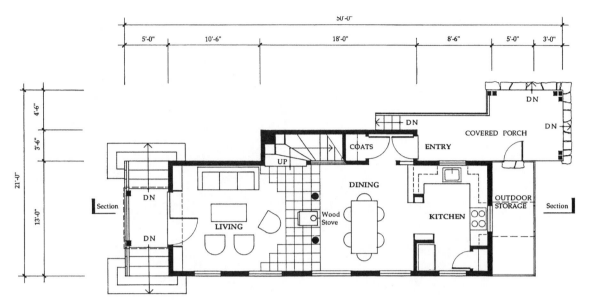

First Floor Plan

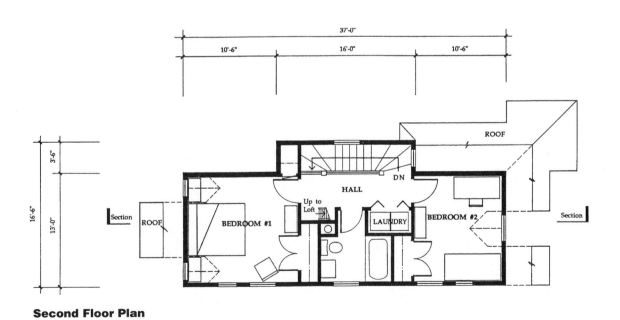

Second Floor Plan

North Elevation

South Elevation

RIDGE

8'-9"

LOFT

8'-0"

2ND

8'-6"

1ST

East Elevation

West Elevation

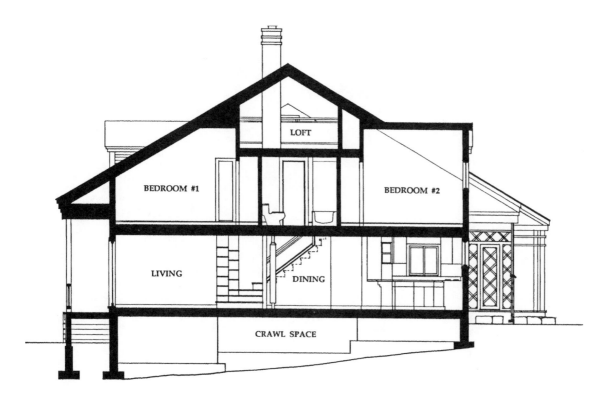

LOFT

BEDROOM #1

BEDROOM #2

LIVING

DINING

CRAWL SPACE

Wall Section

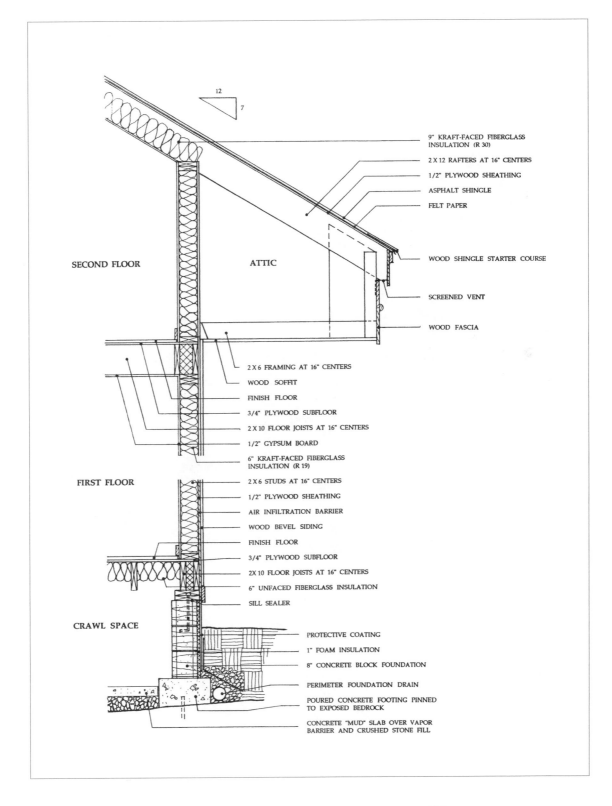

9" KRAFT-FACED FIBERGLASS INSULATION (R 30)

2 X 12 RAFTERS AT 16" CENTERS

1/2" PLYWOOD SHEATHING

ASPHALT SHINGLE

FELT PAPER

WOOD SHINGLE STARTER COURSE

SCREENED VENT

WOOD FASCIA

SECOND FLOOR

ATTIC

2 X 6 FRAMING AT 16" CENTERS

WOOD SOFFIT

FINISH FLOOR

3/4" PLYWOOD SUBFLOOR

2 X 10 FLOOR JOISTS AT 16" CENTERS

1/2" GYPSUM BOARD

6" KRAFT-FACED FIBERGLASS INSULATION (R 19)

FIRST FLOOR

2 X 6 STUDS AT 16" CENTERS

1/2" PLYWOOD SHEATHING

AIR INFILTRATION BARRIER

WOOD BEVEL SIDING

FINISH FLOOR

3/4" PLYWOOD SUBFLOOR

2 X 10 FLOOR JOISTS AT 16" CENTERS

6" UNFACED FIBERGLASS INSULATION

SILL SEALER

CRAWL SPACE

PROTECTIVE COATING

1" FOAM INSULATION

8" CONCRETE BLOCK FOUNDATION

PERIMETER FOUNDATION DRAIN

POURED CONCRETE FOOTING PINNED TO EXPOSED BEDROCK

CONCRETE "MUD" SLAB OVER VAPOR BARRIER AND CRUSHED STONE FILL

Perspective

John

Separating living room by entry courtyard gives a nice space for terrace. Very clean plan. Nice projection over living room and bedroom doors. Clean, simple massing.
PETER WOERNER

I like the clarity, the simplicity, and the rational zoning. This house can be built inexpensively. Best for warmer climes.
DON METZ

Paul Robin John

This house is designed to provide exciting and comfortable living amenities within a small footprint.

The spaces are articulated into two zones defining the various activities of daily life. These zones are expressed as linked volumes containing public and private functions. The foyer, providing the circulation linkage between the two, also contains the mechanical core.

Separating the plan into two basic elements provides a protected central entry courtyard and a covered terrace. These exterior spaces expand the living space visually and literally and create private views inward from most rooms, minimizing exterior openings toward neighbors in close proximity. Sloping sites are also accommodated easily with change of floor levels between elements.

The kitchen is central to both living and family room and is open for ease of service to both areas, and through patio doors to the terrace. Partitions are door height to allow the vaulted ceiling to flow uninterrupted.

Roofs are steeply pitched to create interior volumes and promote air circulation. All exterior door openings are protected by wood trelliswork covered with clear lexan. Windows feature closable Bahama shutters.

Walls can be frame or masonry construction depending upon locale, and exterior and interior material selection may vary within the basic concept of creating simple, crisp forms as a final result.

Paul Robin John

TECHNICAL DATA

Gross Square Feet:
1,248 (house)
448 (terrace and entry)
1,696 (gross)

Location:
Southern United States or Caribbean

Materials:
See wall section drawing

Type:
Masonry or stick-built

Estimated Cost to Build:
$95,000

Estimated Heating/ Cooling Costs:
$1,200 per year

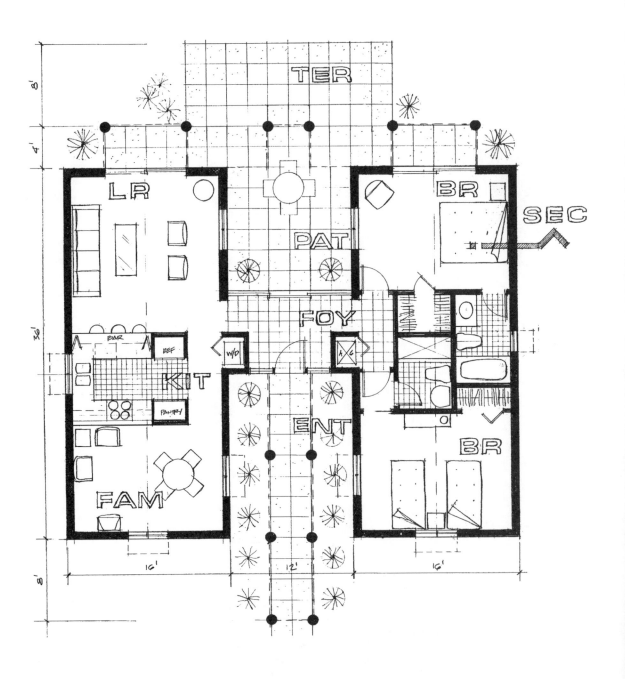

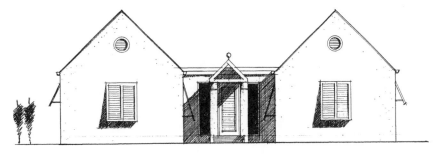

Front Elevation

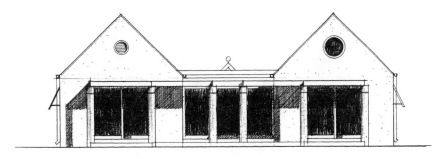

Rear Elevation

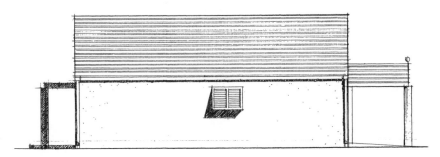

Side Elevation 1

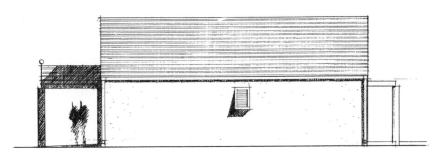

Side Elevation 2

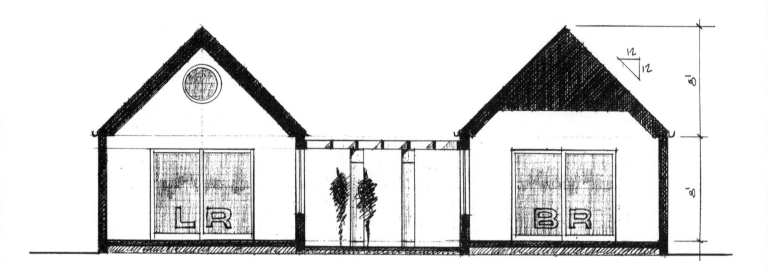

Wall Section

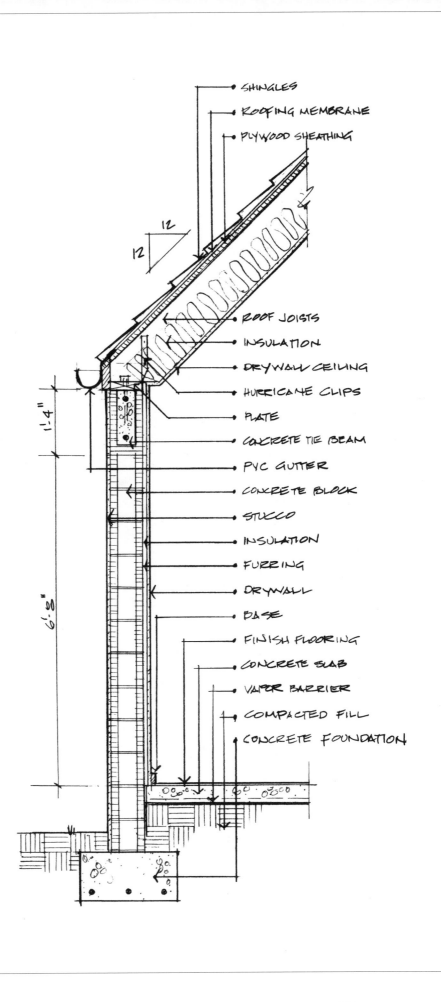

SHINGLES

ROOFING MEMBRANE

PLYWOOD SHEATHING

12
12

ROOF JOISTS

INSULATION

DRYWALL CEILING

HURRICANE CLIPS

PLATE

CONCRETE TIE BEAM

PVC GUTTER

CONCRETE BLOCK

STUCCO

INSULATION

FURRING

DRYWALL

BASE

FINISH FLOORING

CONCRETE SLAB

VAPOR BARRIER

COMPACTED FILL

CONCRETE FOUNDATION

1'-4"

6'-8"

Perspective

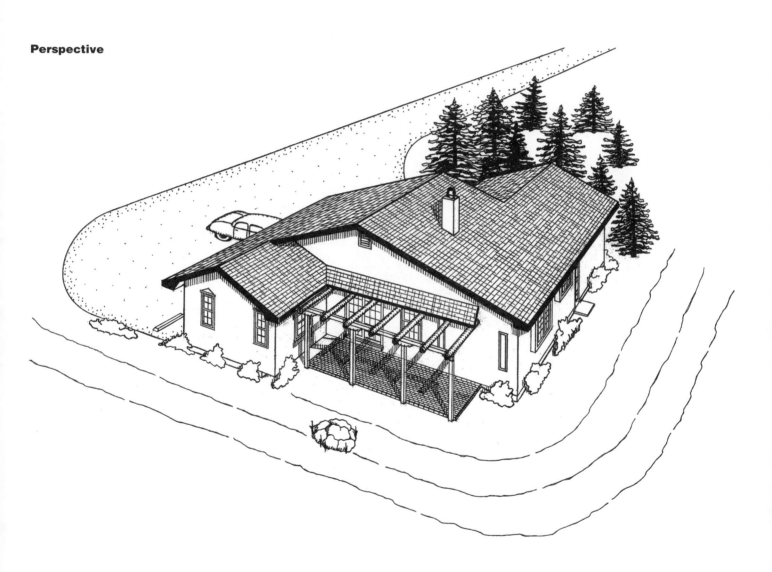

Ludeke

JURY COMMENTS

A classic ranch house design. Easy to build, economical, sensible.
DON METZ

Good big space for living room. Simple ranch treatment.
PETER WOERNER

Nice adaption of the Santa Fe style to a set of different climate and site demands and possibilities.
BEN WATSON

Charles H. Ludeke

Hoping to retire next year, my client intends to build this Santa Fe style home on a 5-acre wooded tract in the Black Forest of Colorado. He expects to do most of the construction himself, with a minimum of hired labor. Therefore, I divided the roof system into three separate trusses to span the 44-foot width, which allowed for the 10-foot ceiling height in the living room and made the trusses easy for two men to handle.

A gabled roof and false beams were substituted for the flat roof and vigas of the conventional Santa Fe home due to the high snow loads in this area. Peeled ponderosa pine logs were used at the front and rear portals, however, as they grow in abundance on the property. Everything was taken into consideration to make this design as simple to build as possible.

Window trim, shutters, doors, base, and casing will be shop-built by the owner in order to follow through on the Southwest style.

With a crawl space there is the option of various heating systems, such as a gas down draft forced-air furnace with metal ductwork, or a "plenwood" system. Another option would be an "in-floor" hot water radiant floor system using poured gyp-crete over plastic pipe.

A good part of the heating requirement will be provided by an efficient zero-clearance fireplace insert, which can be finished with tiles in the traditional manner.

Charles H. Ludeke

TECHNICAL DATA

Gross Square Feet:
1,248

Location:
Black Forest, Colorado
(elevation 7,500 ft.)

Materials:
2"x4" wood frame; Mexican tile in living room; carpeting in bedrooms; stucco exterior; concrete and brick portals

Type:
Traditional stick-built on crawl space foundation

Estimated Cost to Build:
$50,000

Estimated Heating/ Cooling Costs:
N/A

Site Plan

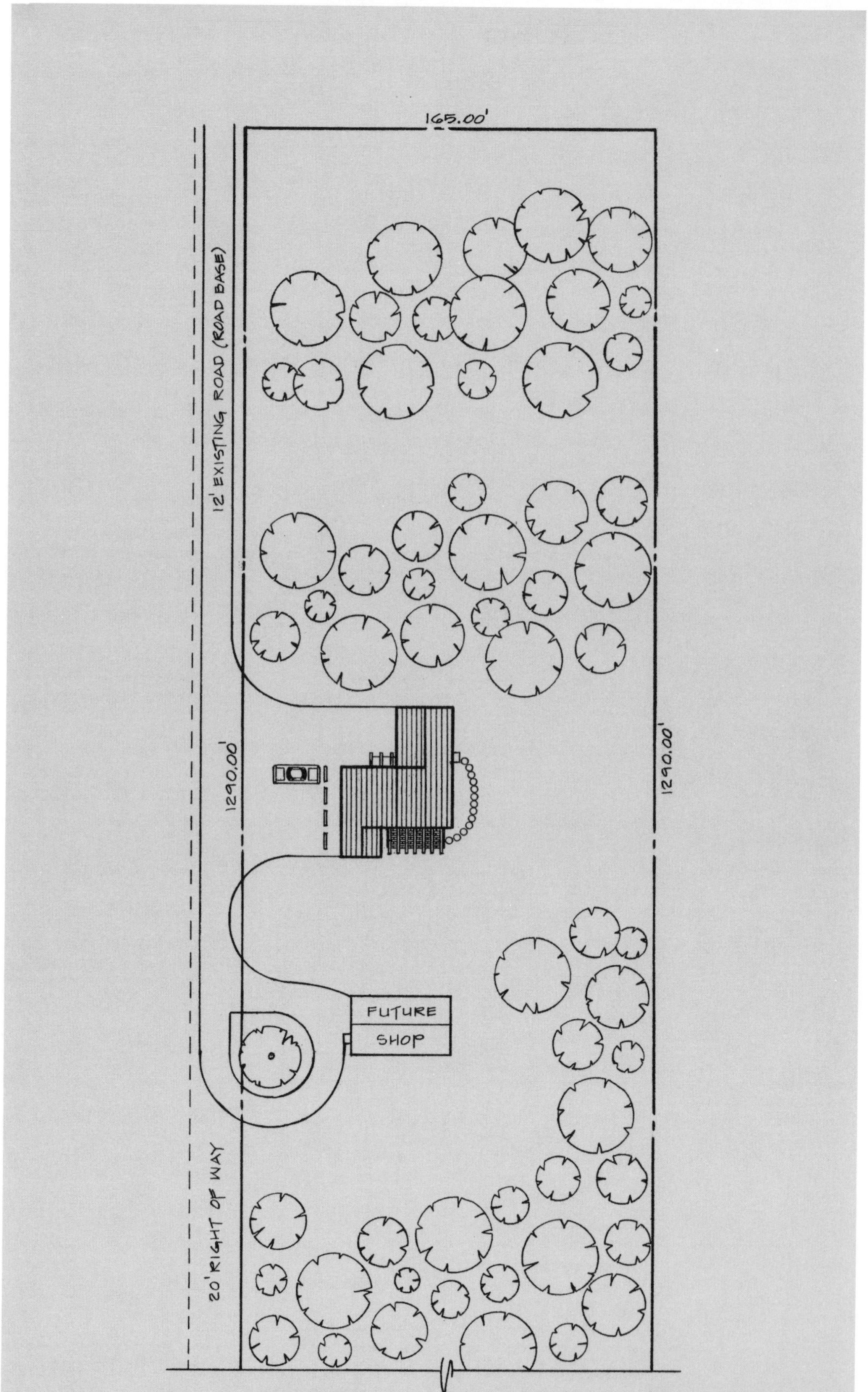

165.00'

12' EXISTING ROAD (ROAD BASE)

1290.00'

1290.00'

20' RIGHT OF WAY

FUTURE SHOP

132

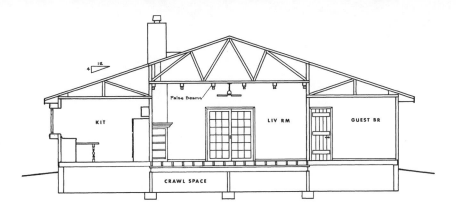

Floor Plan

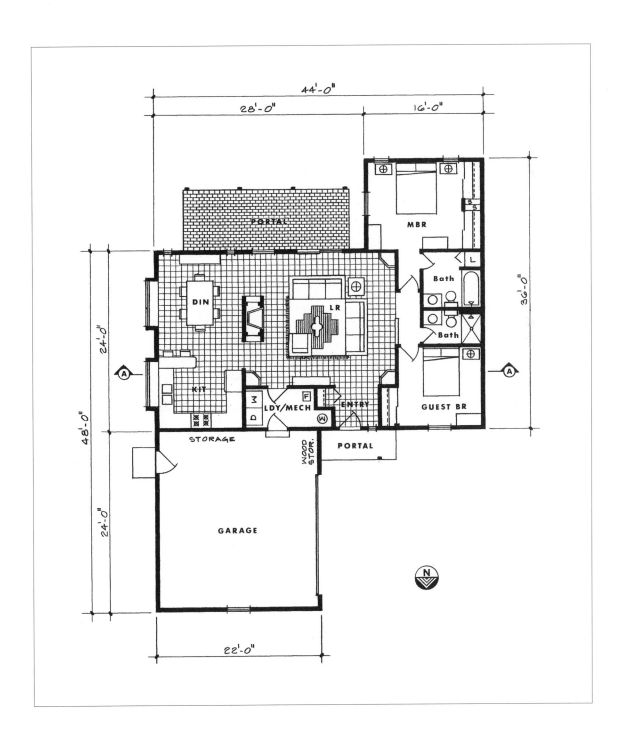

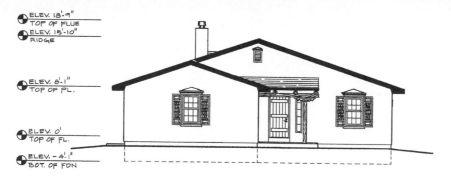

ELEV. 18'-9"
TOP OF FLUE
ELEV. 15'-10"
RIDGE

ELEV. 8'-1"
TOP OF PL.

ELEV. 0'
TOP OF FL.

ELEV. -4'-1"
BOT. OF FDN

North Elevation

South Elevation

East Elevation

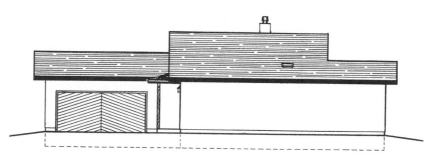

West Elevation

Wall Section

1. 220# fiberglass/asphalt 3-tab shingles over 15# asphalt felt
2. ⁷⁄₁₆" waferboard roof sheathing
3. Double-thick 6" fiberlass batt insulation, installed at 90° to each other for a total of R-38
4. Scarfed 2"x4" trusses @ 24" o.c.
5. ½" gypsum board, taped and "Spanish lace" textured
6. Double 2"x4" top plates
7. 1"x4" #3 spruce continuous ledger
8. ⅜" Cladwood textured soffit
9. 8"x16" G.I. soffit vents
10. 1"x8" primed pine, ⅜" plowed fascia
11. 4"x3" OG galvanized iron gutters connected to 3"x2" rectangular downspouts
12. 2"x4" 92 ⅝" S&B white wood studs at 16" o.c.
13. R-13 fiberglass batt insulation
14. ½" Styrofoam "blue board"
15. 2 coat stucco
16. 2"x4" sole plate
17. 2¼" #0366 oak baseboard
18. ¾" T & G oriented strand board subfloor, glued in joints over joists and nailed; ¼" luan mahogany plywood underlayment stapled over it where tile or vinyl finish floor is used
19. 2"x8" H.F. #2 joists @ 16" o.c.
20. R-19 fiberglass batt insulation
21. 1"x8" #3 spruce rim joist
22. 2"x4" construction common redwood
23. ½" diameter x 10" anchor bolts @ 6'0" o.c. (max.)
24. 8"x41" poured concrete stem wall
25. 2 - #4 grade 60 rebar at top and bottom
26. 3"x8" cardboard voids or footers as per engineer
27. 30# asphalt felt, lapped and sealed
28. Brown coat stucco
29. Finished grade
30. Compacted earth fill
31. Sand
32. 36" - 6 mil black visqueen mopped to wall and carried under drain
33. Pea gravel
34. 4" perforated ADS pipe to daylight

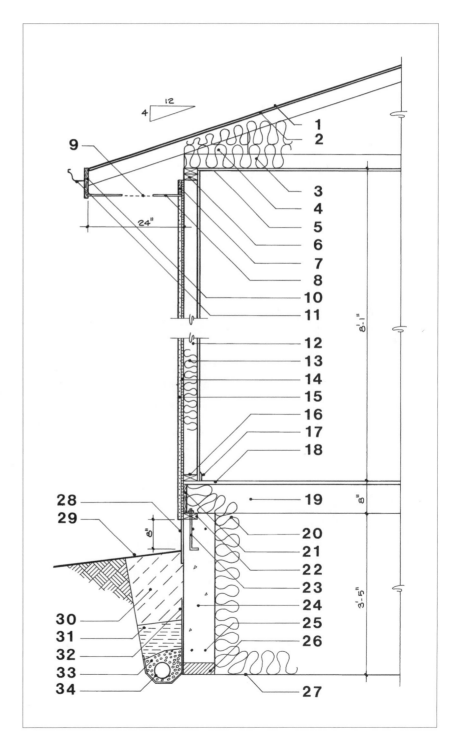

Perspective

Luderowski

JURY COMMENTS

An enormous amount of house for so few square feet. A rural "camp" feel to the elevations. Easily expandable.

DON METZ

I like the ordered simplicity of this house. The two axes on the first floor organize and define spaces. At the same time, they are not just corridors, but have other uses — stairs, kitchen counter, and the little study/sleeping area. The fenestration has a classic simplicity. At first glance, the house has a cabin/camp feel to it, but it is much more. The foundation could easily be changed to a perimeter foundation with crawl space or basement. Good clean simple lines.

PETER WOERNER

Nils Luderowski

This camp building, located in New York State's Adirondack Park, was developed for a club that was founded in 1890. The building is one of several new prototype camps to be proposed for new development on 1- to 3-acre lots. Most existing buildings in the club were built between 1890 and 1930; some atypical structures/remodels were built in later years.

The new camps must be dissimilar and yet also similar to existing vintage camps. They must be honest in their construction methods and try to capture the spirit of the club and its relationship to its natural surroundings. Camps will be built as either summer or year-round dwellings.

SITE/CONSTRUCTION

Sites are on a variable degree slope on the western shore of Lake Champlain, overlooking the lake and the mountains on the opposite shore. The site for the specific design shown is on the shoreline, with an average slope of 10 percent.

In its most economical and simple form, the building shall have a pole/cast pier foundation, 2"x6" wall framing with prefabricated 2"x6" monoplaner wood trusses and asphalt shingle roofing. (No "second floor." Open to window on second level for air and light; summer use only.) Insulation optional. The fully equipped winterized version would have a masonry foundation with full basement, 2"x6" wall framing,

TECHNICAL DATA

Gross Square Feet:
1,230

Location:
Western shore of Lake Champlain, New York State (elevation 152 ft.; 8,000 +/- degree days)

Materials:
1½-story, light wood frame construction on concrete piers; standing seam metal roof; wood clapboard siding; PTW trellis skirting

Mechanical Systems:
Well-insulated envelope; R-25 walls, R-30/40 ceiling, R-30 floors; hydronic heating with wood backup/assist; natural gravity ventilation

Estimated Cost to Build:
BASIC VERSION:
$90,000 (cast piers, shingle siding, asphalt shingle roof, undeveloped attic)

CUSTOM VERSION:
$140,000 (continuous frostwall, wood clapboard siding, standing seam metal roof, developed attic)

Estimated Heating/ Cooling Costs:
$300 to $600 per heating season

and a 1½-story roof truss with a standing seam metal roof. Both versions have lapboard or cedar shingle siding. Various options in the treatment of porches, dormers, and fenestration are available within the concept.

INTERIOR CONSIDERATIONS

Interior functions are grouped in four quarters: entry; utility; food preparation; laundry, dining, living, and sleeping.

For summer use, "porch walls" fold away and screens are installed on first-floor porches. By opening all casement windows, combined spaces form one large "porch."

Two axis paths form a direct pattern of circulation, also providing alternate access and privacy, all at the discretion of the dweller.

The long paths, with framed views at each end, and the upper dormer lights, along with interior walls selectively terminating at 6 feet, 6 inches, allow awareness of nature, time, and light at all times of the day, perhaps giving an illusion of grandeur in a very small and humble building.

Nils Luderowski

**Winter-Use and
Light Diagram**

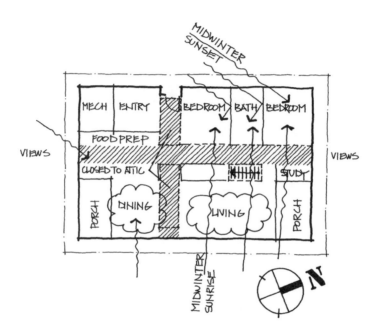

**Summer-Use and
Light Diagram**

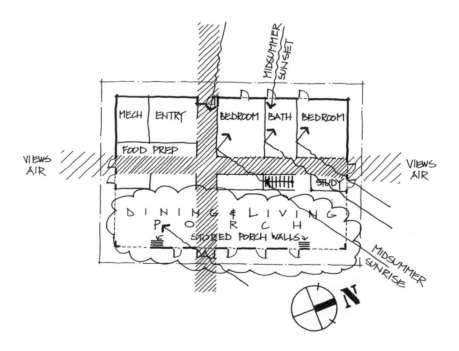

First Floor Plan

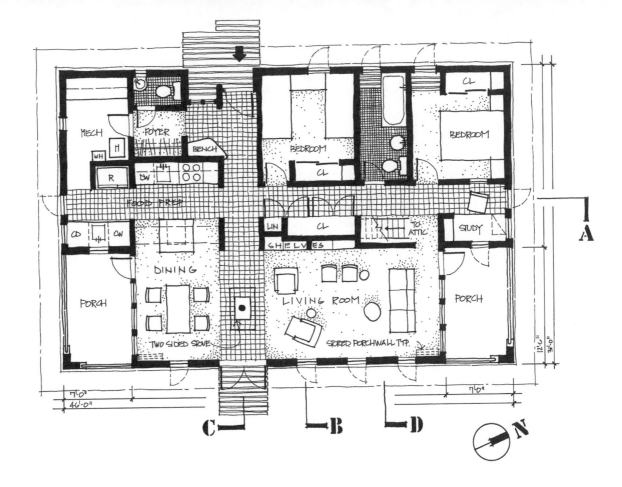

Attic Floor Plan

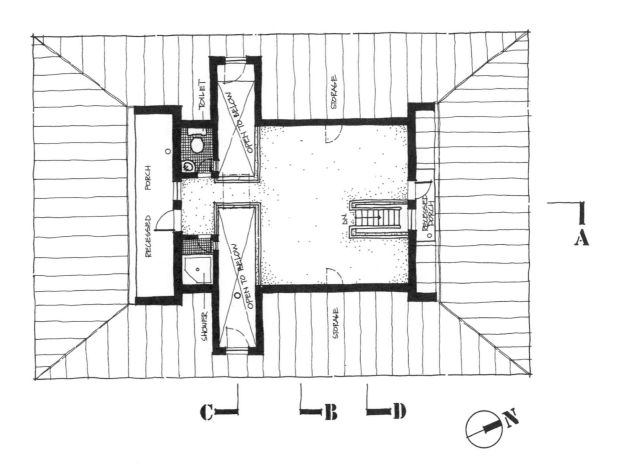

East Elevation

West Elevation

South Elevation

Site Plan

LAKE CHAMPLAIN NEW YORK

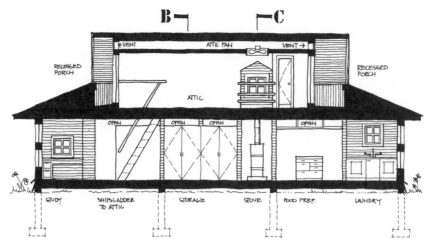

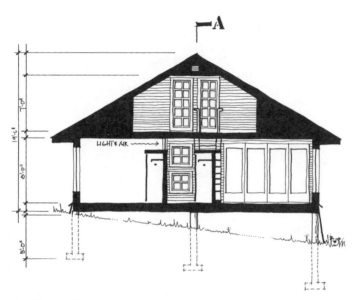

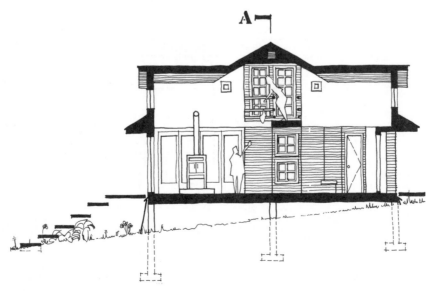

Section A-A

Section B-B

Section C-C

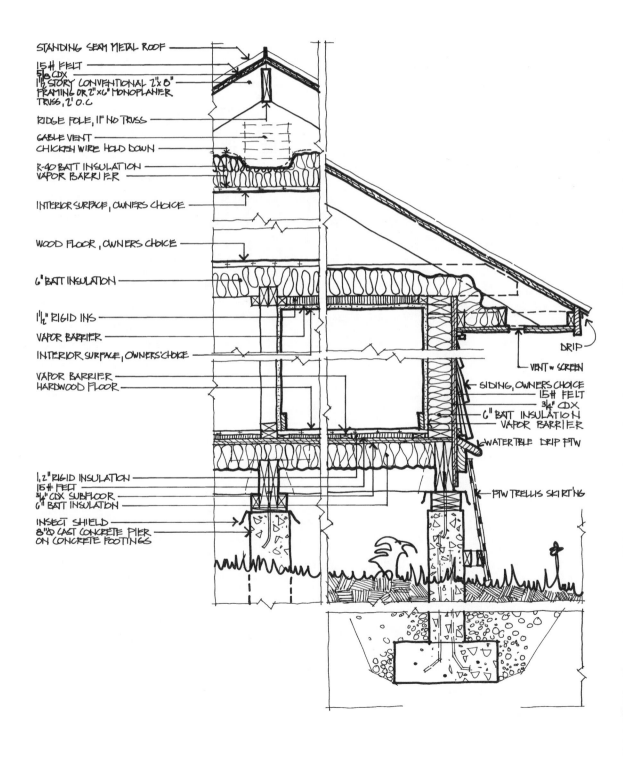

STANDING SEAM METAL ROOF

15# FELT
5/8 CDX
1½ STORY CONVENTIONAL 2"x 8"
FRAMING OR 2"x6" MONOPLANER
TRUSS, 2' O.C

RIDGE POLE, IF NO TRUSS

GABLE VENT
CHICKEN WIRE HOLD DOWN

R-40 BATT INSULATION
VAPOR BARRIER

INTERIOR SURFACE, OWNERS CHOICE

WOOD FLOOR, OWNERS CHOICE

6" BATT INSULATION

1½" RIGID INS

VAPOR BARRIER

INTERIOR SURFACE, OWNERS' CHOICE

VAPOR BARRIER
HARDWOOD FLOOR

1,2" RIGID INSULATION
15# FELT
¾" CDX SUBFLOOR
6" BATT INSULATION

INSECT SHIELD
8"Ø CAST CONCRETE PIER
ON CONCRETE FOOTINGS

DRIP

VENT w/ SCREEN

SIDING, OWNERS CHOICE
15# FELT
¾" CDX
6" BATT INSULATION
VAPOR BARRIER

WATERTBLE DRIP PTW

PTW TRELLIS SKIRTING

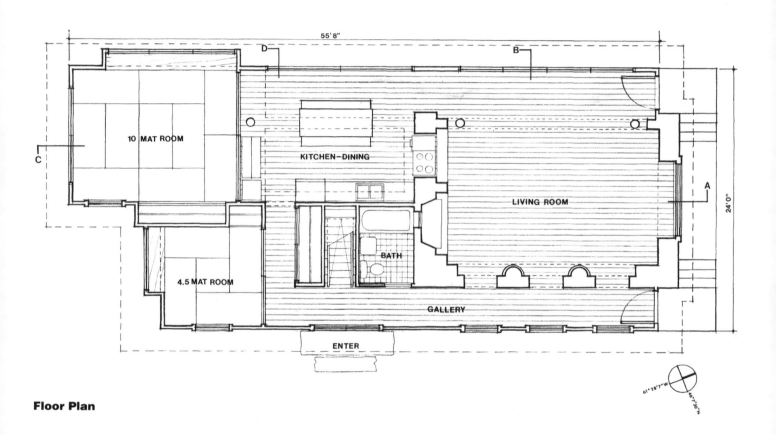

Floor Plan

Nishi

JURY COMMENTS

Nishi's design combines a potpourri of elements, from tatami to Neoclassical temple to Gothic to today — and it works wonderfully.
DON METZ

Strong integrating blend of Japanese and traditional forms. Wonderful sense of openness.
PETER WOERNER

Geoff K. Nishi

This compact house was designed for a scholar and an artist to serve as their summer workplace, in addition to fulfilling the functions of dwelling.

The design is a synthesis of rural Japanese and colonial Maritime vernacular architectural traditions conceived within the context of contemporary North American culture, climate, and construction. The traditional forms of two cultures have been appropriated due to the efficiency of the living patterns that they support. Traditional materials and construction have been augmented with contemporary energy technology to provide extreme durability and economy.

The house is located in a bowl surrounded on three sides by low mountains and the ocean to the west. The landscape is a patchwork of soft- and hardwood forest, old subsistence farm fields, and well-spaced, century-old farmhouses. The internal functions are distributed according to their relationship with specific views and orientations: ocean sunsets to the west; a close garden to the south; the old farmhouse framed by mountains and the northern lights to the north; and an orchard, a stream, and forest climbing toward the sunrise.

The house is to be heated with wood. The massive stone walls act as a thermal storage bank and radiator, allowing the house to be unoccupied for four days in the most severe weather. Exposed stone is protected by a quilt of insulation fastened to the exterior during the months of December, January, and February.

This design may be adapted to take maximum advantage of any site by rearranging the ancillary functions about the main space and service core. In addition, the generic concept can accommodate unlimited programmatic variation.

Geoff K. Nishi

TECHNICAL DATA

Gross Square Feet:
1,230

Location:
Cape Breton Island, Nova Scotia, Canada

Materials:
Local granites; local hard- and softwood timbers, decking, and boards

Type:
Masonry; heavy and medium timber structure with clapboard and frame and panel interior and exterior finishes.

Estimated Cost to Build:
$60,000 (Canadian)

Estimated Heating/ Cooling Costs:
8 cords hardwood ($480 Canadian)

Project assistance from Tom Brozovic, Cissy Wong, Annetta Massie, and Ken Nishi

East Porch

EAST PORCH

West Veranda

WEST VERANDA

North Porch

NORTH PORCH

South Face

SOUTH FACE

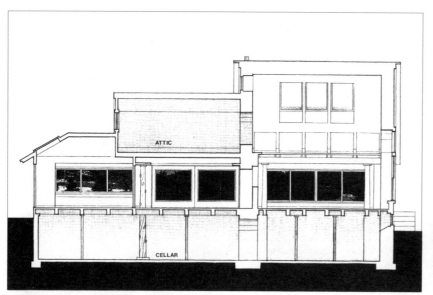

Section A-A — Sunset Views

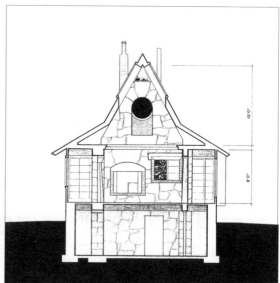

Section B-B — Hearth Elevation

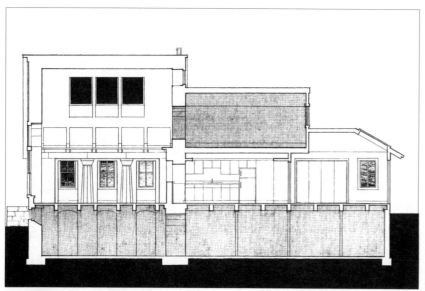

Section C-C — Sunrise Views

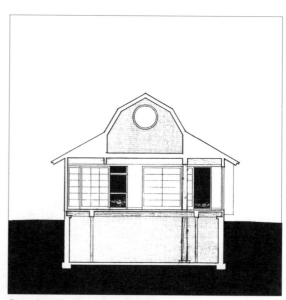

Section D-D — Garden Views

Wall Section

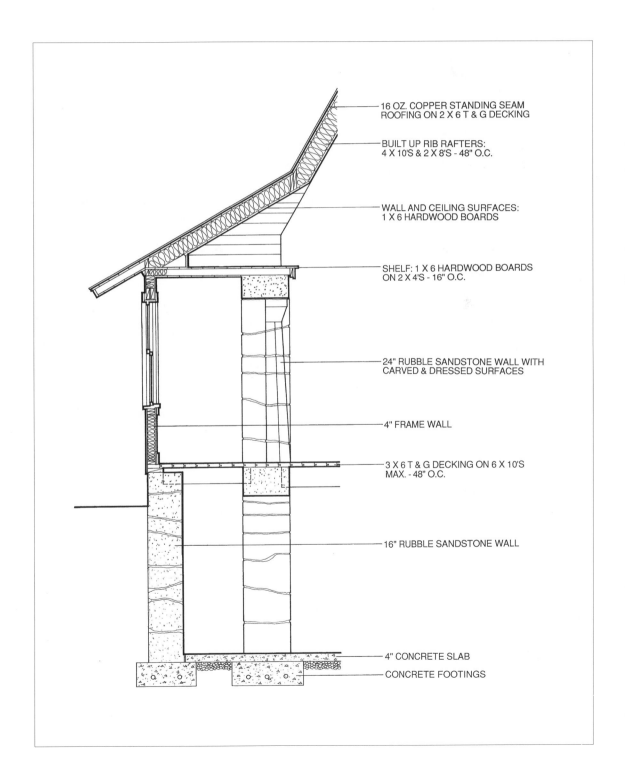

16 OZ. COPPER STANDING SEAM
ROOFING ON 2 X 6 T & G DECKING

BUILT UP RIB RAFTERS:
4 X 10'S & 2 X 8'S - 48" O.C.

WALL AND CEILING SURFACES:
1 X 6 HARDWOOD BOARDS

SHELF: 1 X 6 HARDWOOD BOARDS
ON 2 X 4'S - 16" O.C.

24" RUBBLE SANDSTONE WALL WITH
CARVED & DRESSED SURFACES

4" FRAME WALL

3 X 6 T & G DECKING ON 6 X 10'S
MAX. - 48" O.C.

16" RUBBLE SANDSTONE WALL

4" CONCRETE SLAB

CONCRETE FOOTINGS

149

Perspective

Nugent

JURY COMMENTS

Classic New England lines and materials make this house pleasingly familiar, comfortable out in the country or in the village.
DON METZ

Good composition. The scale of the exterior is done well.
PETER WOERNER

Nancy Nugent

BRATTLEBORO HOUSE

This house is modeled after a typical New England farmhouse and is intended for either an infill lot in a small city or for a more rural setting. A private and protected patio and garden is formed by the house and garage as shown, or without the garage with a fence. The front porch provides a more public outdoor area. An unheated vestibule creates an airlock to keep heat in during the winter and to maintain a cooler environment in the summer.

The plan is a simple central entry hall flanked by a room to either side on each floor. There is a full basement below where the mechanical systems are located. The heating system shares a chimney with the zero-clearance fireplace flue in the chimney as shown by the minimal masonry chimney.

Of 6-inch insulated wood frame construction, the house is sided with 6-inch clapboard wood siding or with 6-inch beaded flush wood siding and finished with two coats of a deep base stain. The roof is cedar shakes. The windows have true divided lights, and double-pane glass.

The design of this house is generated from the geometry of the golden section. Thus, all elements, from the smallest detail to the entire plan and elevation, are unified. Although its proportioning system is not obvious, this house will evoke in all who experience it a sense of beauty and perfection, despite its modesty and practicality.

Nancy Nugent

TECHNICAL DATA

Gross Square Feet:
1,225

Location:
Northeastern United States

Materials:
Wood frame construction; concrete footings and foundation; 6" clapboard wood siding (or 6" beaded flush wood siding); cedar shake roofing

Estimated Cost to Build:
1,225 sq. ft. @ $80.00/sq. ft. = $98,000

Estimated Heating/ Cooling Costs:
N/A

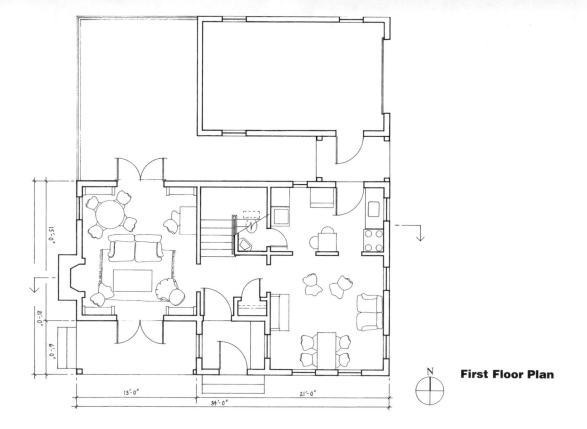

First Floor Plan

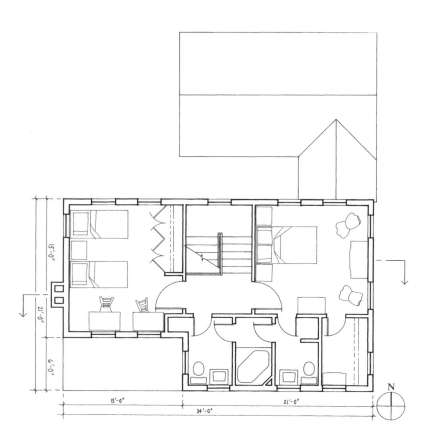

Second Floor Plan

East Elevation

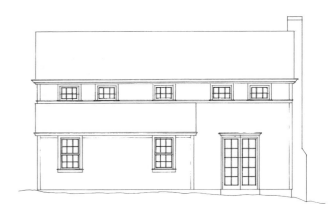

North Elevation

South Elevation

West Elevation

Wall Section

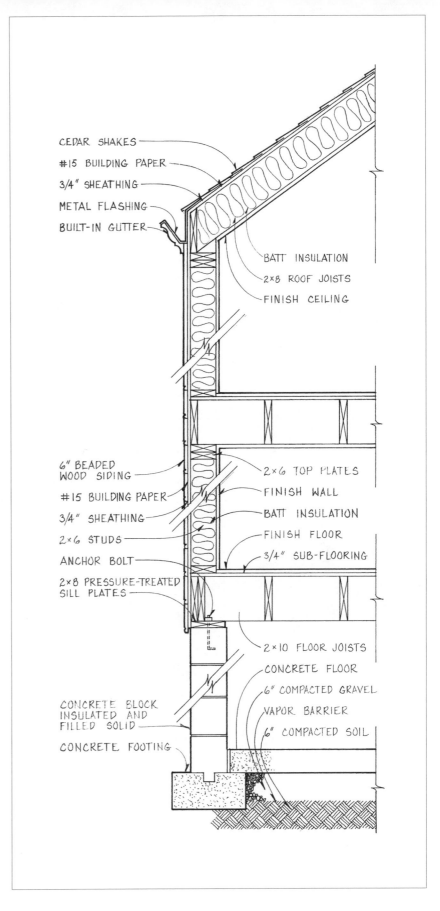

CEDAR SHAKES

#15 BUILDING PAPER

3/4" SHEATHING

METAL FLASHING

BUILT-IN GUTTER

BATT INSULATION

2×8 ROOF JOISTS

FINISH CEILING

6" BEADED WOOD SIDING

#15 BUILDING PAPER

3/4" SHEATHING

2×6 STUDS

ANCHOR BOLT

2×8 PRESSURE-TREATED SILL PLATES

2×6 TOP PLATES

FINISH WALL

BATT INSULATION

FINISH FLOOR

3/4" SUB-FLOORING

2×10 FLOOR JOISTS

CONCRETE FLOOR

6" COMPACTED GRAVEL

VAPOR BARRIER

6" COMPACTED SOIL

CONCRETE BLOCK INSULATED AND FILLED SOLID

CONCRETE FOOTING

Perspective

Rahman

JURY COMMENTS

Askew plan — gives interesting spaces. Living room and dining room for urban space.
PETER WOERNER

Handsome street facade. Perfect for urban infill housing. I like the skewed axis and the trapezoidal rooms.
DON METZ

Atiqur Rahman

This compact house is designed for a tropical climate, but it might be implemented with little modification anywhere in the world where justified by the site, access, orientation, etc.

The elevations are simple geometric forms: a rectangle with a vaulted roof, a cube with a pitched roof, square openings, terraces, and an external stair make for varied perspectives from different angles. The whole building is framed by a free-standing column with beam, which creates a homogeneous facade in the urban context.

The most important aspects of this design are the interior circulation, the definition of space (private, semiprivate, public, etc.), and the sequence of space according to its function. The flow of space, the openness of the design, and the different levels create a cozy, intimate home environment.

Landscape design would depend upon the size of the plot, the client's requirements or preferences, the available budget, and many other factors. In fact, terraces could be used for small-size plantings and orchids could be grown on walls within the frame to give the effect of a mural or relief.

The basic concept of the design is to create an environment that is comfortably liveable, easy to build, economical, and that at the same time has a certain degree of architectural quality.

Atiqur Rahman

TECHNICAL DATA

Gross Square Feet:
1,050

Location:
Dhaka, Bangladesh

Materials:

STRUCTURAL:
Concrete column beam

WALLS:
Brick, metal stud/gypsum wallboard

FLOOR:
Carpeting/concrete slab/vct.

ROOF:
Brick, ceramic tile

Estimated Cost to Build:
1,050 sq. ft. @ $140.00/sq. ft. = $147,000 (includes site improvement)

Estimated Heating/ Cooling Costs:
N/A

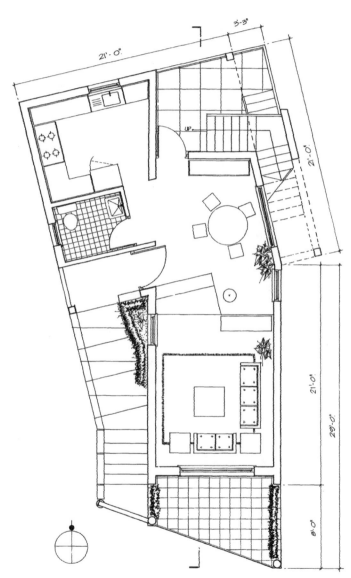

First Floor Plan

Second Floor Plan

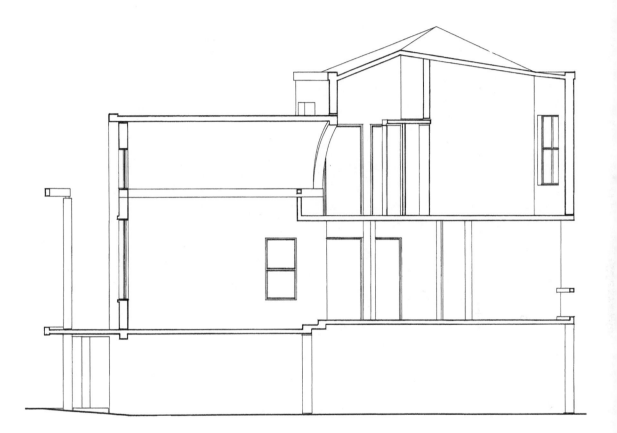

South Elevation

East Elevation

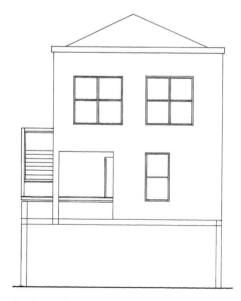

North Elevation

Wall Section

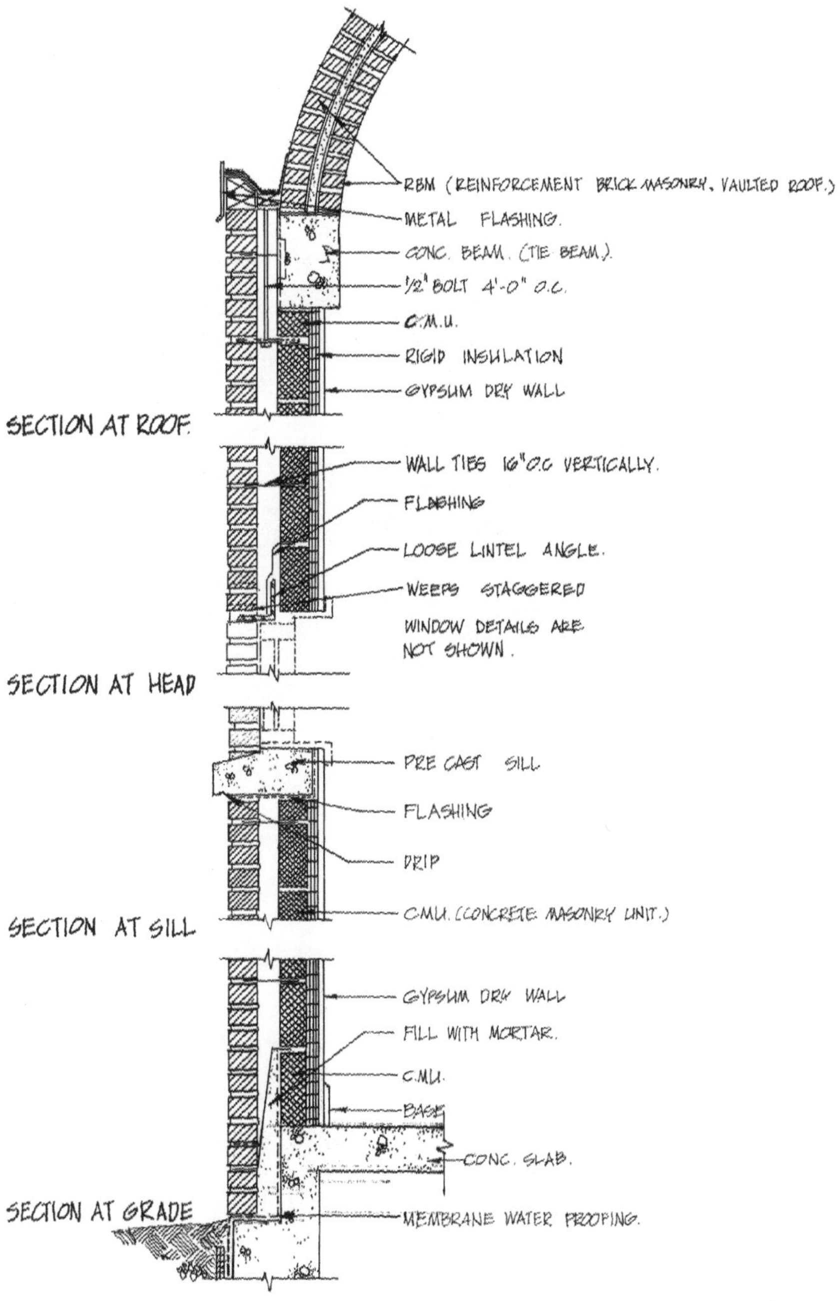

RBM (REINFORCEMENT BRICK MASONRY, VAULTED ROOF.)
METAL FLASHING.
CONC. BEAM. (TIE BEAM.)
½" BOLT 4'-0" O.C.
C.M.U.
RIGID INSULATION
GYPSUM DRY WALL

SECTION AT ROOF.

WALL TIES 16" O.C VERTICALLY.
FLASHING
LOOSE LINTEL ANGLE.
WEEPS STAGGERED
WINDOW DETAILS ARE NOT SHOWN.

SECTION AT HEAD

PRE CAST SILL
FLASHING
DRIP
C.M.U. (CONCRETE MASONRY UNIT.)

SECTION AT SILL

GYPSUM DRY WALL
FILL WITH MORTAR.
C.M.U.
BASE
CONC. SLAB.
MEMBRANE WATER PROOFING.

SECTION AT GRADE

161

Perspective

Raskin

Good relationship to terrace. Large living room — sense of openness and verticality to living room area. A little overbearing with the Postmodern exterior.
PETER WOERNER

Highly stylized facades. Floor plan enhanced by two-story spaces.
DON METZ

Lisa Raskin

Approaching this house from the east, the expansive, linear porch suggests, not a "compact" house, but a large home. This initial perception is carried through the inside of the house with the manipulation of form and space. Through this manipulation the "typical" compact house, often dominated (out of necessity) by function, becomes a creative integration of aesthetics with the functional, cost-saving requirements.

While designing a functional living environment, several significant factors were given special consideration: the zoning of public versus private spaces, circulation, and the relationship between the house and its site. I believe that the identity of each room is very important, especially in a small residence. Therefore this house is zoned so that the majority of the circulation occurs at the central entry corridor, providing access to each public room. The layout was devised to minimize traffic through the

public spaces in order to allow the living room, for instance, to be perceived as a "place." The stairway is a major source of vertical circulation as it provides access to the second floor and roof terrace, as well as to the basement (where the utilities are located). I found that a "cubist" sort of approach to circulation generated an appropriate sense of movement and spatial playfulness through the house.

The relationship between building and natural environment played a key role in my design. The beauty of the Upper Peninsula shorelines is equalled by the harshness of the winters. From a functional standpoint, the large south-facing glass wall in the dining room and window in the living room allow the sun to warm the main living space while providing uninterrupted views to the lake and orchard. North-facing windows have been minimized. The fireplace is centrally located and is open to both the living and dining rooms. The house is primarily heated by a

TECHNICAL DATA

Gross Square Feet:
1,250 (excluding basement and garage)

Location:
Small inland lake shoreline, Upper Peninsula, Michigan (elevation 677 ft.; 7,000 degree days)

Materials:
Cast-in-place concrete foundation walls; wood frame; built-up wood roof and galvalume roof; pine siding; hardwood floors

Type:
Superinsulated, light wood frame construction

Estimated Cost to Build:
$85,000

Estimated Heating/ Cooling Costs:
$1,000 (excluding fireplace)

high-efficiency furnace and is superinsulated to effectively reduce heating bills.

Formally, the harmonious balance between the house and its site goes beyond the use of pine siding, hardwood floors, and a "formalized nautical/ lighthouse" style by incorporating several porches, a large terrace, a second-floor balcony, and a roof garden. With these "expansions" the house begins to embrace the landscape as it pulls the outside in and extends the area of the house to include the natural environment.

Lisa Raskin

Alternate Perspective (with Garage)

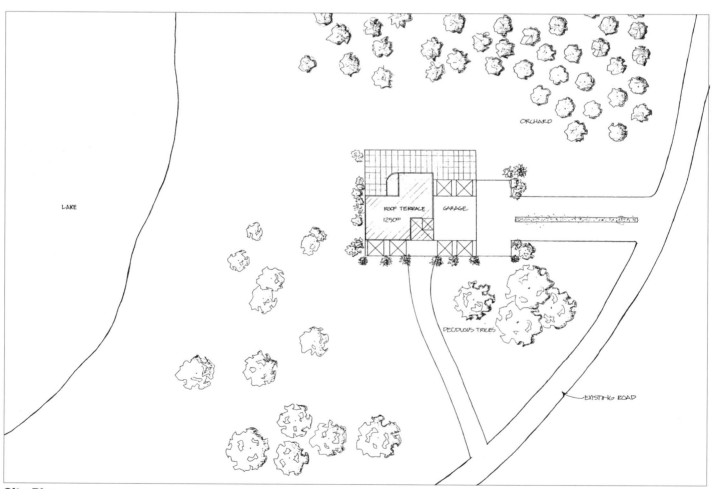

Site Plan

First Floor Plan

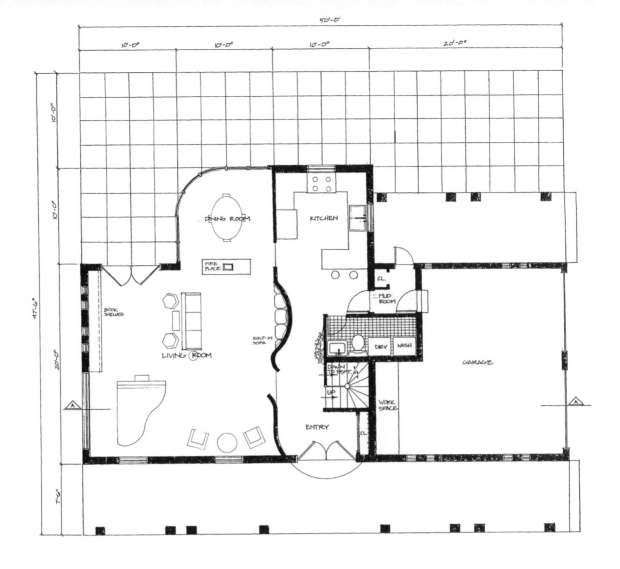

50'-0"

10'-0"   10'-0"   10'-0"   20'-0"

10'-0"

10'-0"

47'-6"

20'-0"

7'-6"

DINING ROOM

KITCHEN

FIRE PLACE

CL.

MUD ROOM

BOOK SHELVES

BUILT-IN SOFA

LIVING ROOM

DRY   WASH

DOWN TO BSMT.

UP

GARAGE

WORK SPACE

ENTRY

CL.

Second Floor Plan

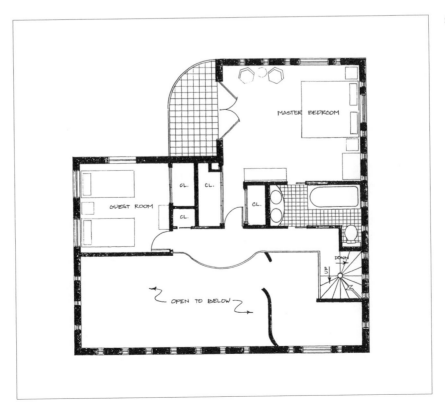

MASTER BEDROOM

GUEST ROOM

CL.   CL.

CL.

CL.

CL.

DOWN

UP

OPEN TO BELOW

165

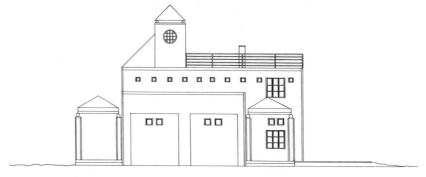

North Elevation

South Elevation

East Elevation

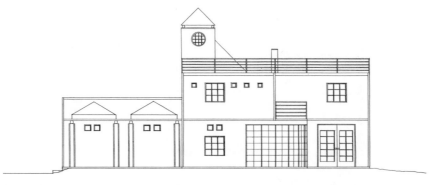

West Elevation

Wall Section

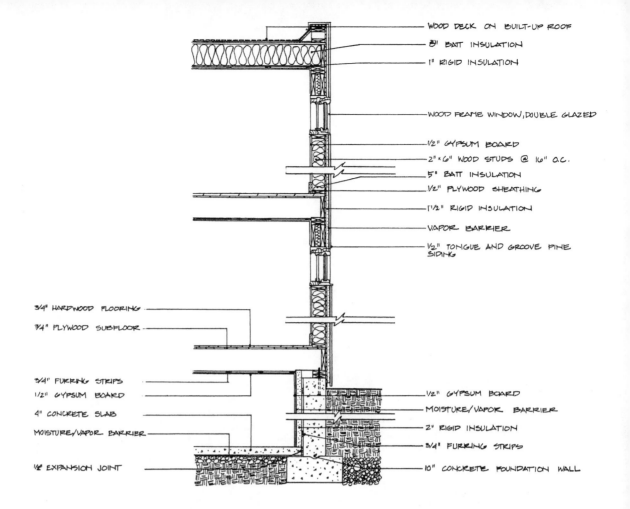

WOOD DECK ON BUILT-UP ROOF

8" BATT INSULATION

1" RIGID INSULATION

WOOD FRAME WINDOW, DOUBLE GLAZED

1/2" GYPSUM BOARD

2"x6" WOOD STUDS @ 16" O.C.

5" BATT INSULATION

1/2" PLYWOOD SHEATHING

1 1/2" RIGID INSULATION

VAPOR BARRIER

1/2" TONGUE AND GROOVE PINE SIDING

3/4" HARDWOOD FLOORING

3/4" PLYWOOD SUBFLOOR

3/4" FURRING STRIPS

1/2" GYPSUM BOARD

4" CONCRETE SLAB

MOISTURE/VAPOR BARRIER

1/2" EXPANSION JOINT

1/2" GYPSUM BOARD

MOISTURE/VAPOR BARRIER

2" RIGID INSULATION

3/4" FURRING STRIPS

10" CONCRETE FOUNDATION WALL

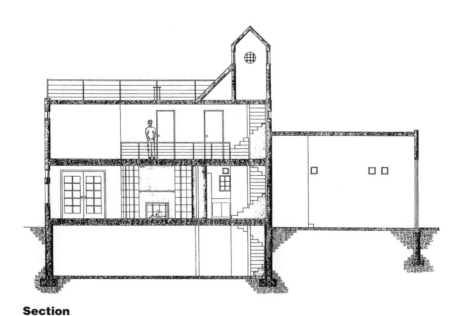

Section

167

Perspective

Rutkowski

JURY COMMENTS

An audacious application of an Elizabethan facade to a contemporary floor plan. Not inexpensive. A brick mason's challenge.
DON METZ

Nice scale breakdown on facade. Great open plan. Add bath for second floor. Good entry.
PETER WOERNER

Thomas Rutkowski

This compact house was designed to be sensitive to contemporary living, yet maintain traditional elegance at the same time. Though cottage-like, there's an aura of stateliness to the exterior appearance. Traditional materials such as brick, wood, and stucco are combined to form a contemporary timber-framed house. Contrary to traditional Tudor-style homes, which use heavy, dark timbers, this design uses timbers that are lighter, both in weight and color.

In keeping with the sophistication of the exterior, the interior projects a formal sense combined with casual living capabilities. Upon entering the house, you're greeted by a stair hall with a cathedral ceiling and a balcony overlook. From here, a narrow pas-

sageway opens up into a large living area. The primary living space is comprised of the living room, dining room, and kitchen — all of which contribute to a spacious "great room" atmosphere since there are no partition walls.

Upstairs, a loft hallway looks down on the grand living room fireplace. The second-floor bedroom is cozy with clipped ceilings leading to an octagonal lookout cupola. The master bedroom and bath are richly proportioned with high ceilings, generous storage, and large floor space. This compact house offers the characteristics of a large home with the intimacy of a smaller one.

Thomas Rutkowski

TECHNICAL DATA

Gross Square Feet:
1,250

Location:
Suburban

Materials:
Timber frame, stucco and brick

Estimated Cost to Build:
N/A

Estimated Heating/ Cooling Costs:
N/A

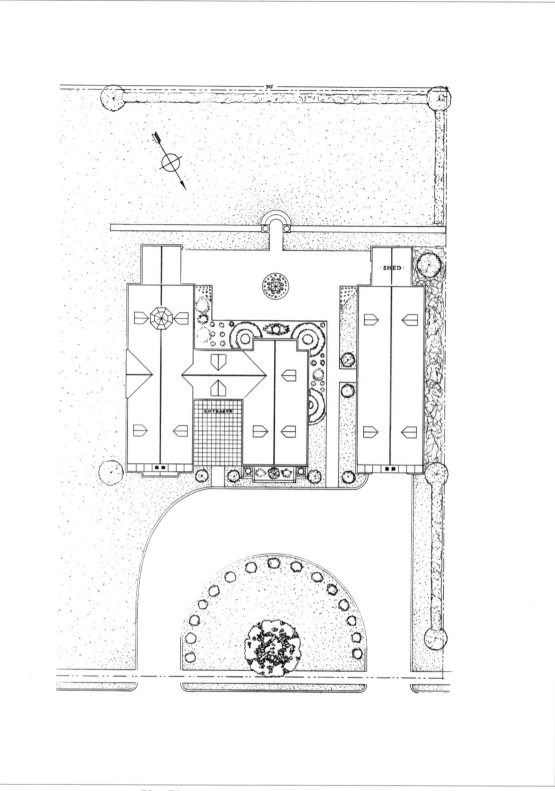

Site Plan

First Floor Plan

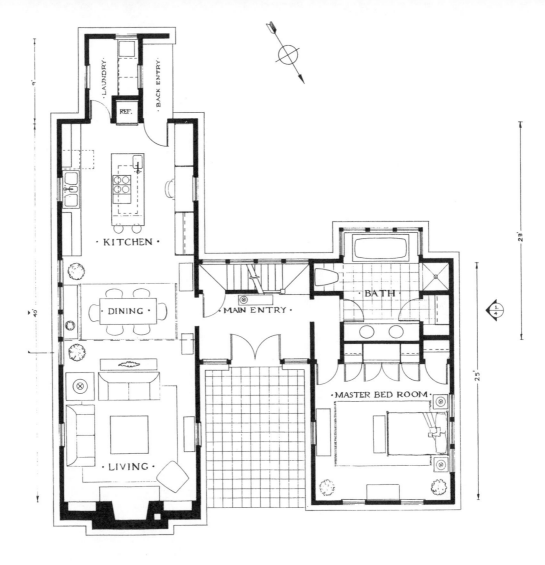

- LAUNDRY -
- BACK ENTRY -
REF.
- KITCHEN -
- DINING -
- MAIN ENTRY -
BATH
- MASTER BED ROOM -
- LIVING -

Second Floor Plan

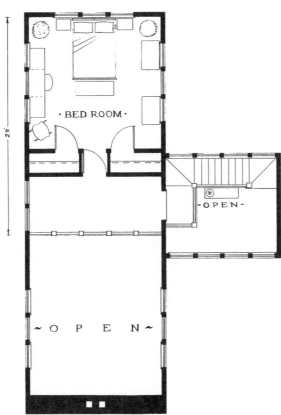

- BED ROOM -
~ O P E N ~
~ O P E N ~

Side Elevation 1

Front Elevation

**Optional Garage
with Studio Above**

Rear Elevation

Side Elevation 2

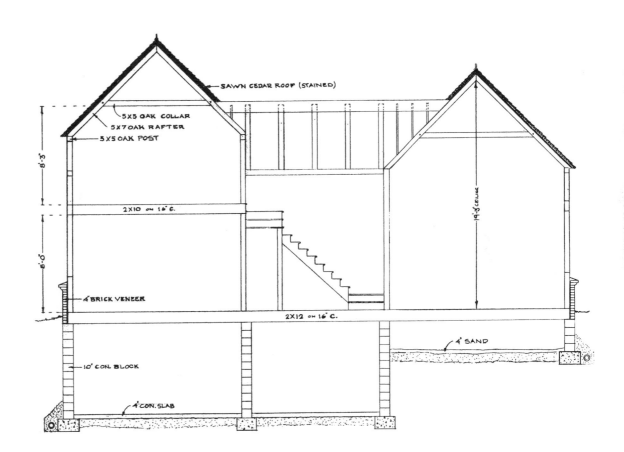

SAWN CEDAR ROOF (STAINED)

5X5 OAK COLLAR

5X7 OAK RAFTER

5X5 OAK POST

8'-3"

2X10 on 16" C.

8'-0"

4" BRICK VENEER

2X12 on 16" C.

19'-3" CEILING

4" SAND

10" CON. BLOCK

4" CON. SLAB

Section

Perspective

Utt

JURY COMMENTS

A well-wrought miniature version of the classic Yankee farmhouse. North side entry and south side porch establish appropriate public/private realms.
DON METZ

Very simple, straightforward, economical.
PETER WOERNER

Tim Utt

This house is designed for a site in east-central Vermont, in the upper Connecticut River valley. Though designed for the cold climate of the Northeast, the plan also offers protection from the summer sun.

The design was inspired by the traditional homes of Vermont. Steeply pitched roofs, clapboard siding, and 1½-story construction were some of the elements I used to create a home for a family on a limited budget.

The house is balloon-framed, in two 16-foot-wide sections, forming a T-shaped structure. Along the south face, a porch and a breakfast bay project. Vertically, the house is divided into three levels. A poured concrete basement houses mechanical

utilities, laundry, and wood and tool storage. The first floor is public space with work areas to the west and the living room to the east. The second floor has two bedrooms, a bath, and an office/bedroom.

Fifty percent of the house's windows face south to maximize solar gain. The porch and breakfast bay allow sun to enter but keep glaring winter sunlight off work spaces. A wood stove heats the house comfortably on 3 cords per year. A second chimney flue allows the option of a basement furnace.

This house is designed as a buildable, energy-efficient structure, retaining the massing, materials, and details of traditional Vermont homes.

Tim Utt

TECHNICAL DATA

Gross Square Feet:
1,250

Location:
Central Vermont

Materials:
Poured concrete foundation; wood frame; standing seam metal roof

Type:
Stick-built

Estimated Cost to Build:
$75,000

Estimated Heating/ Cooling Costs:
$300 (3 cords hardwood @ $100/cord))

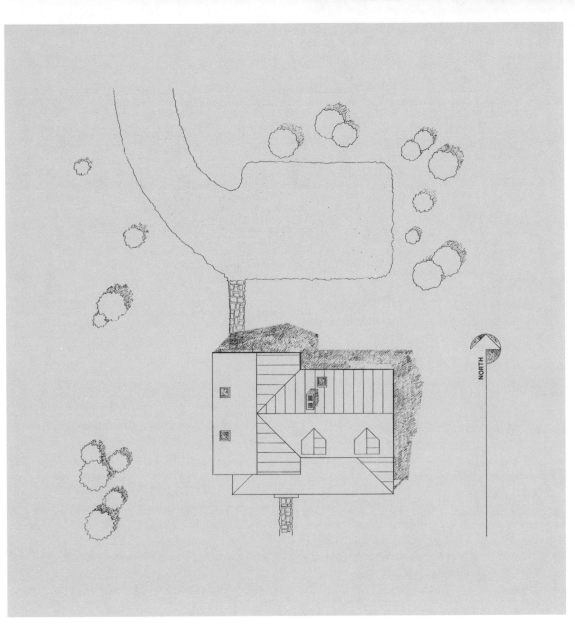

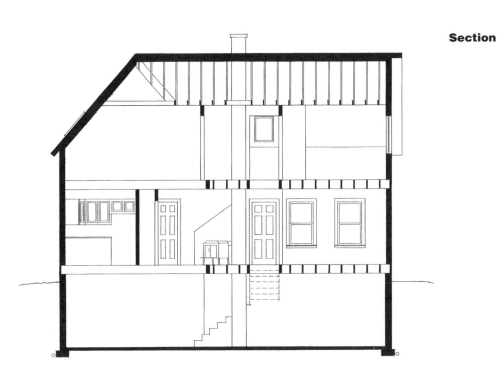

First Floor Plan

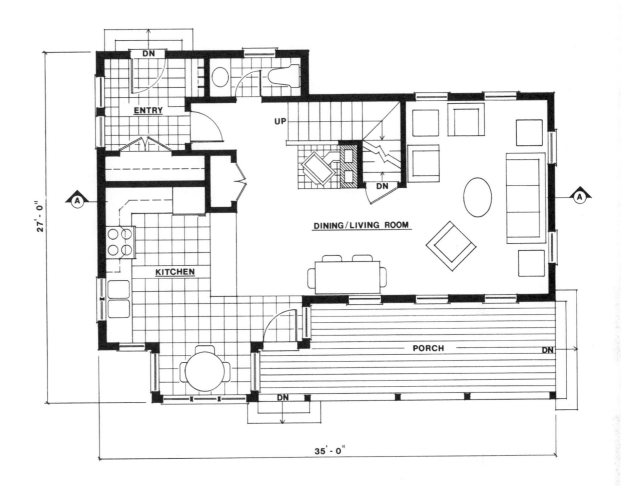

27' - 0"

35' - 0"

DN

ENTRY

UP

DN

DINING/LIVING ROOM

KITCHEN

PORCH

DN

DN

A

A

Second Floor Plan

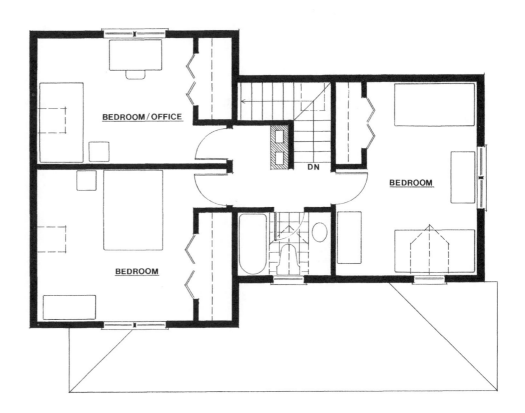

BEDROOM/OFFICE

DN

BEDROOM

BEDROOM

North Elevation

South Elevation

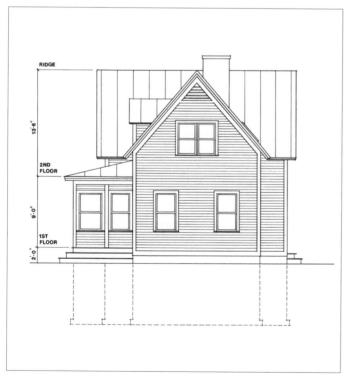

RIDGE

13'-6"

2ND
FLOOR

9'-0"

1ST
FLOOR

2'-0"

East Elevation

West Elevation

Wall Section

1. Standing seam metal roof
2. 15 lb. felt paper
3. L" CDX plywood roof sheathing
4. 2"x10" rafters
5. 1"x8" and 1"x4" roof trim
6. Continuous soffit vent strip
7. 1"x10" soffit
8. 1"x6" frieze board
9. Cedar clapboards
10. Typar housewrap
11. H" CDX wall sheathing
12. 2"x12" floor joist
13. 2"x4" firestop
14. 4"x6" header
15. 1"x4" window trim
16. Double-hung window
17. 2"x6" stud
18. R-19 fiberglass insulation
19. 2"x12" band joist
20. 2"x12" floor joist
21. 1"x8" water table board
22. 2"x8" p.t. sill
23. Stucco foundation coat
24. 2" Styrofoam blueboard insulation
25. 8" poured concrete foundation
26. Topsoil
27. Gravel backfill
28. Crushed stone
29. 4" perforated drain pipe
30. R-38 fiberglass insulation
31. 2"x6" collar tie
32. 4 mil vapor barrier
33. H" Sheetrock
34. R-30 fiberglass insulation with proper vents
35. 1" Styrofoam blueboard insulation
36. 1"x3" strapping
37. 2"x6" top and double plates
38. 4 mil vapor barrier
39. H" Sheetrock
40. I" T & G plywood underlayment
41. H" Sheetrock
42. 2"x8" joist support
43. 4"x6" sill
44. I" T & G plywood underlayment
45. Concrete footing
46. 4" concrete slab
47. 4 mil vapor barrier
48. 2" Styrofoam blueboard insulation
49. 6" compacted gravel
50. Undisturbed earth

Perspective

Watson

JURY COMMENTS

A house for all seasons and most neighborhoods. Compact American styling. The idea of optional elevations is appealing.
DON METZ

Nice open plan. The greenhouse/solarium is not easily accessible.
PETER WOERNER

Donald Watson

The Ecology House design is a plan designed in collaboration with the New Alchemy Institute of East Falmouth, Massachusetts, as an affordable "starter home" that is energy-efficient and environmentally wise. The basic plan is a 26'x26' footprint that creates 1,035 square feet (net usable floor space), with an optional 162-square-foot greenhouse/airlock. To make the most of the small footprint, the foundation is provided with optional windows, large enough to allow future completion of the lower level for additional living space/bedrooms, where south sunlight and the earth-berming effect of the ground provide year-round comfort.

The home is designed for maximum energy efficiency for North American temperate and cold climates (above 40° latitude). Energy-efficient specifications include high insulation standards, south-facing windows and greenhouse, and an optional

solar hot water system. The double-height living room and open stair provide a simple means by which solar heat is distributed throughout the house. Clerestory windows allow winter sun to reach throughout the interior. The south-facing windows are shaded in summer.

The plan allows three options for arranging the living, dining, and kitchen areas, either as separate areas or combined as a "great room." The greenhouse option — also earth-bermed — provides space for an interior working garden or a sun room/family room. Outside the greenhouse is a wind-protected sun patio. The design is easily adapted to flat or sloped sites and can also be used with attached housing in duplex and triplex arrangements.

Donald Watson

TECHNICAL DATA

Gross Square Feet:
1,035 (plus 162 sq. ft. greenhouse); additional 520 sq. ft. available if basement is finished as usable living space

Location:
North American temperate to cold climates (above 40° latitude)

Materials:
2"x6" wood frame construction (also adaptable to stress-skin panel construction or post and beam construction)

Estimated Cost to Build:
$96,000 without greenhouse; $112,000 with greenhouse

Estimated Heating/Cooling Costs:
Less than $100 per year for heating if built with recommended energy-efficient specifications in Hartford, Connecticut, climate and if using a solar hot water system; no cooling costs. An air-circulating fan is recommended year-round (estimated cost of $20.00

per month), but this can be powered by photovoltaic energy.

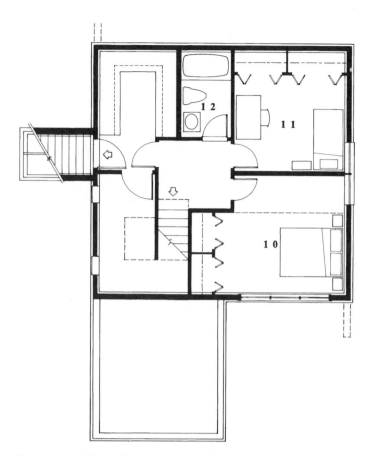

Basement Plan (Future Options)

625 SF

162 SF

First Floor Plan

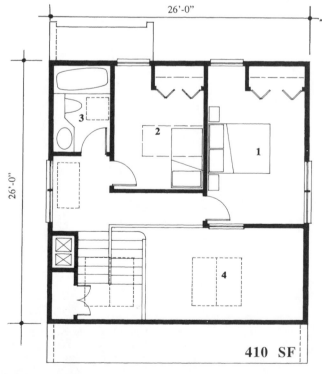

26'-0"

26'-0"

410 SF

Second Floor Plan

Plan Option (Kitchen on South)   **Plan Option (Kitchen and Dining)**

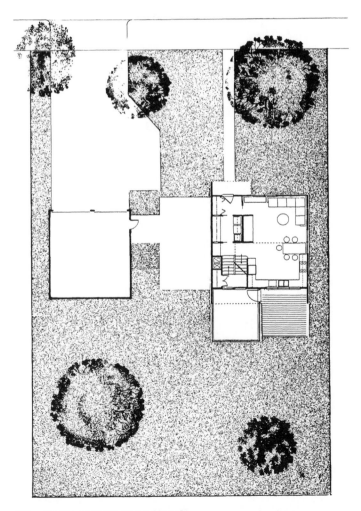

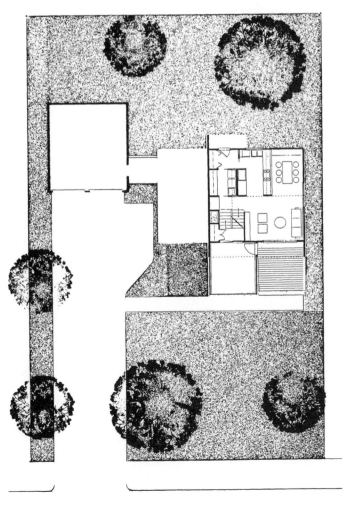

Site Options/Street to North   **Site Options/Street to South**

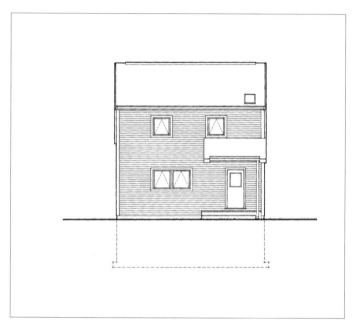

North Elevation

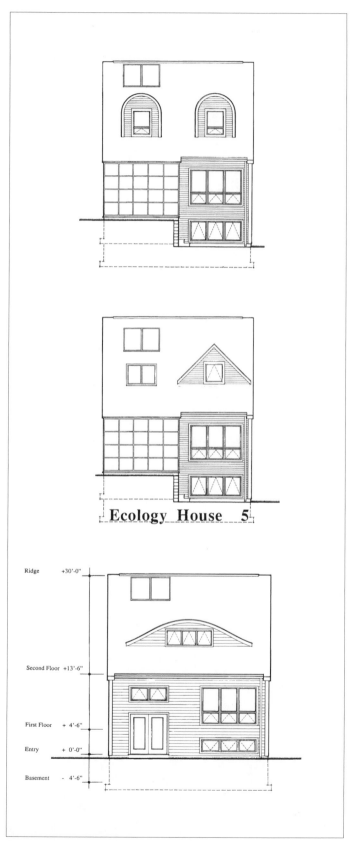

Ecology House 5

Ridge   +30'-0"

Second Floor +13'-6"

First Floor   + 4'-6"

Entry   + 0'-0"

Basement   - 4'-6"

South Elevation (Various Options)

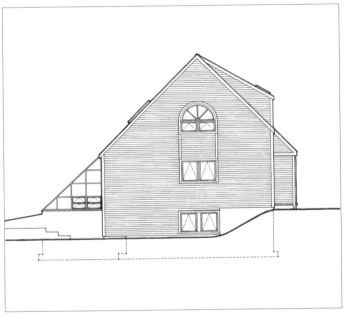

East Elevation

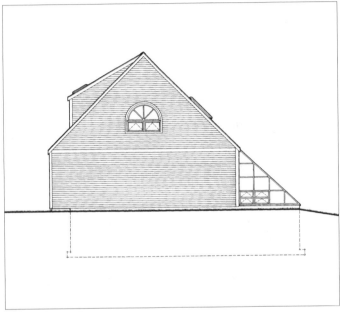

West Elevation

Multi-Family Option (Attached)

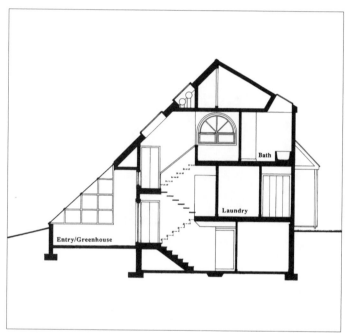

Section through Stairwell

Section through Living Room/Kitchen

Wall Section

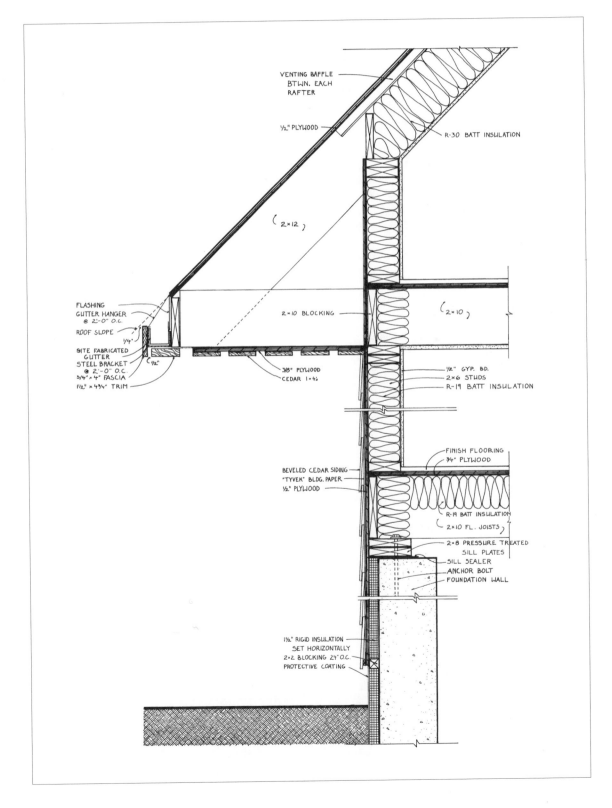

VENTING BAFFLE
BTWN. EACH
RAFTER

½" PLYWOOD

R-30 BATT INSULATION

(2×12)

FLASHING
GUTTER HANGER
@ 2'-0" O.C.

ROOF SLOPE
¼"

SITE FABRICATED
GUTTER
STEEL BRACKET
@ 2'-0" O.C.
¾" × 4" FASCIA
1½" × 4¾" TRIM

2×10 BLOCKING

(2×10)

4½"

⅜" PLYWOOD
CEDAR 1×4½

½" GYP. BD.
2×6 STUDS
R-19 BATT INSULATION

BEVELED CEDAR SIDING
"TYVEK" BLDG. PAPER
½" PLYWOOD

FINISH FLOORING
¾" PLYWOOD

R-19 BATT INSULATION
2×10 FL. JOISTS

2×8 PRESSURE TREATED
SILL PLATES
SILL SEALER
ANCHOR BOLT
FOUNDATION WALL

1½" RIGID INSULATION
SET HORIZONTALLY
2×2 BLOCKING 24" O.C.
PROTECTIVE COATING

04/41

Readers interested in obtaining further information on any of the plans featured in this book should contact the appropriate architect or designer directly using the addresses listed below. Fees for working drawings and specifications will vary, and the publisher, Storey Communications, Inc., assumes no financial interest in, or responsibility for, the work of the individuals selected in this design competition.

As a condition of entry for the Second Compact House Competition, the architects and designers listed below have agreed to provide Storey Communications, Inc. with updated address information, which will be included in subsequent printings of this book. If you are unable to reach any architect or designer at the printed address, write to:

Storey Communications, Inc.
Schoolhouse Road
Pownal, VT 05261
ATTN: Compact House Design Information

Readers can also locate architects through the American Institute of Architects (AIA), 1735 New York Avenue, NW, Washington, DC 20006.

Richard B. Ferrier (page 2)
School of Architecture
Box 19108
University of Texas at Arlington
Arlington, TX 76019

Rammed Earth Works (page 8)
P.O. Box 5006
Napa, CA 94581

Primitivo Emilio Conde (page 16)
5933 SW 147 Place
Miami, FL 33193

Nancy Nugent (pages 24 and 150)
11 West 11th Street
New York, NY 10011

Frederick Phillips (page 30)
53 West Jackson Boulevard
Chicago, IL 60604

Richard Sammons (page 38)
111 Bank Street
New York, NY 10014

Gerard Bolsega (page 44)
2832 Grand Boulevard
Highland, IN 46322

Jeffrey Burton (page 50)
2251 Canal Street
Oviedo, FL 32765

Michael Clark Connor (page 56)
28 Chaplin Street
Chaplin, CT 06235

James M. Corkill (page 64)
1720 Sandalwood Drive
Norman, OK 73071

David B. DiCicco (page 72)
School of Design
College of Architecture and
Environmental Design
Arizona State University
Tempe, AZ 85287-2105

Michael J. Fritschij (page 78)
2220 DeVries Avenue
Winnipeg, Manitoba
R2E 0E7 Canada

Daniel Grandy (page 84)
Department of Architecture
Ohio State University
189 Brown Hall (190 West 17th
Avenue)
Columbus, OH 43210

David A. Harris (page 92)
DHT^2 Architecture/Interiors
P.O. Box 483
Spokane, WA 99210

Thomas McClellan Haskell
(page 100)
26 Ralston Avenue
Hamden, CT 06517

J. Whitney Huber (pages 108
and 116)
Box 441
Essex, CT 06426

Paul Robin John (page 124)
1335 2nd Street
Sarasota, FL 34236

Charles H. Ludeke (page 130)
7185 Shoup Road
Black Forest, CO 80908

Nils Luderowski (page 136)
66 West Broadway
New York, NY 10007

Geoff K. Nishi (page 144)
95 Hickory Hill
Tappan, NY 10983

Atiqur Rahman (page 156)
902 44th Street, D-7
Brooklyn, NY 11219

Lisa Raskin (page 162)
604 Lakewood Lane
Marquette, MI 49855

Thomas Rutkowski (page 168)
431 Walnut Street
Spring City, PA 19475

Tim Utt (page 174)
P.O. Box 153
Old Turnpike Road
South Strafford, VT 05070

Donald Watson (page 180)
2 Irving Place
Troy, NY 12180